WINGS OF
AIR AMERICA

Terry Love

Schiffer Military/Aviation History
Atglen, PA

ACKNOWLEDGMENTS

Frank Bonansinga, Tom Hansen, Philip Chinnery, Bob Livingstone, Dr. Larry Sall, Al Adcock, Robert Mikesh, Larry LaVerne, Ward Reimer, Jim Rhyne, Captain Frederick F. Walker, John Stallman, President, Air America Association, Jesse Walton, George Stubbs, Wayne Mutza, and Nick Watters III

DEDICATION

To all past Air America employees, and the 243 that did not return, this book is humbly dedicated. I salute you all! A job well done. You all can be justly proud.

Book Design by Ian Robertson.

We are interested in hearing from authors with book ideas on related topics.

Published by Schiffer Publishing Ltd.
4880 Lower Valley Road
Atglen, PA 19310
Phone: (610) 593-1777
FAX: (610) 593-2002
E-mail: schifferbk@aol.com
Please write for a free catalog.
This book may be purchased from the publisher.
Please include $3.95 postage.
Try your bookstore first.

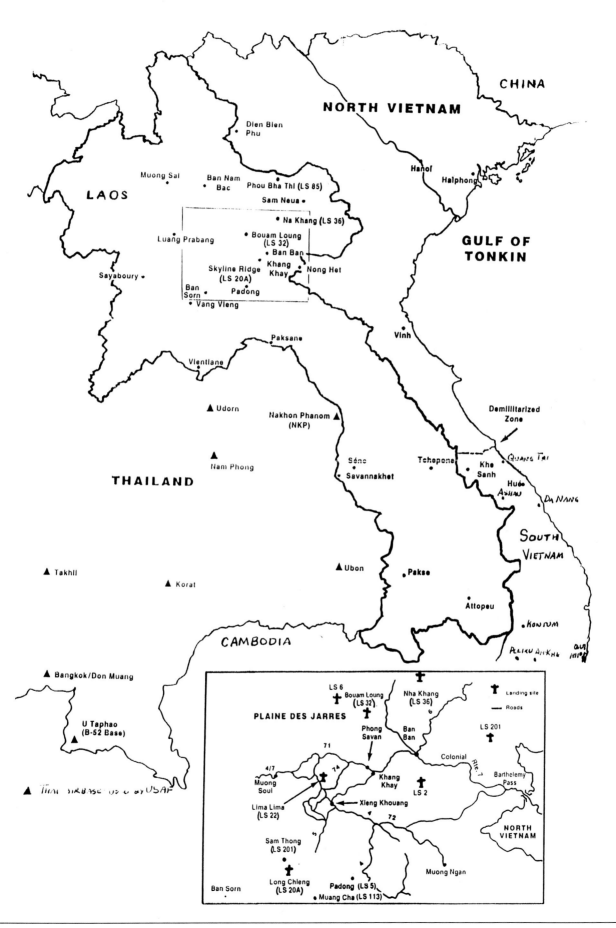

CHINA

NORTH VIETNAM

Dien Bien
Phu

Hanoi

Halphong

LAOS

Muong Sai

Ban Nam
Bac

Phou Bha Thi (LS 85)

Sam Neua

GULF OF
TONKIN

Na Khang (LS 36)

Luang Prabang

Bouam Loung
(LS 32)

Ban Ban

Khang
Khay

Nong Het

Skyline Ridge
(LS 20A)

Sayaboury

Ban
Sorn

Padong

Vang Vieng

Paksane

Vinh

Vientiane

▲ Udorn

Nakhon Phanom
(NKP) ▲

Demilitarized
Zone

▲
Nam Phong

Séno

Savannakhet

Tchepone

Quang Tri

Khe
Sanh

Huế
Ashau

THAILAND

Da Nang

SOUTH
VIETNAM

▲ Takhli

▲ Korat

▲ Ubon

Pakse

Kontum

Attopeu

▲ Bangkok/Don Muang

CAMBODIA

Pleiku Ankhe

Qui
Nhon

U Taphao
(B-52 Base) ▲

▲ Thai Airbase used by USAF

LS 6

Bouam Loung
(LS 32)

Nha Khang
(LS 36)

✝ Landing site
— Roads

PLAINE DES JARRES

Phong
Savan

Ban
Ban

LS 201

Colonial

4/7

71

74

Khang
Khay

LS 2

Rte 7

Barthelemy
Pass

Muong
Soul

Lima Lima
(LS 22)

Xieng Khouang

72

NORTH
VIETNAM

Sam Thong
(LS 201)

Muong Ngan

Ban Sorn

Long Chieng
(LS 20A)

Padong (LS 5)

Muang Cha (LS 113)

INTRODUCTION

The story of Air America actually began in mainland China in April of 1937, when a career U.S. Army Air Corps Captain retired after 20 years of service as a fighter pilot. He served in World War I and in the peacetime Air Corps. He was partially deaf, and had wrinkled skin from years in open-cockpit biplane fighters. This Captain was a man who always seemed to be marching to the beat of a different drummer. He was very passionate in his beliefs and commitments, and frequently stepped on the toes of his superiors. He was a military rebel and a maverick. Therefore, his career languished, but he did lots of flying of pursuit aircraft, and was *the* expert in the area of fighters and tactics. Immediately upon his retirement, he obtained a three-month contract to make a confidential survey of the Chinese Air Force. While conducting this survey, China and Japan began full-scale war. He volunteered his services to the Nationalist government, and he assumed duties with an Air Force that his survey had revealed to be in deplorable conditions. He started a flight training school in Kunming, China, to begin to rebuild the Chinese Air Force. The Chinese were a very backward people at the time, and not very technically inclined. Therefore, this retired captain had to bring in some fellow Americans to help in flight instruction, maintenance, etc. The retired captain was Claire Lee Chennault, and his fellow Americans were the American Volunteer Group, or the AVG, which was better known as the Flying Tigers.

Chennault may have been a thorn in the side of his American superiors, but his relationship with Chiang Kai-Shek remained excellent from then on, because he deferred political decisions to the Generalissimo, showing no interest in China's internal politics.

When America entered World War II after the Pearl Harbor attack by the Japanese, it was decided by the U.S. War Department in Washington, D.C., that the Flying Tigers should lose their identity as an aerial guerilla force and be inducted into the U.S. Army Air Forces as the 23rd Fighter Group. The 23rd Fighter Group still exists today.

The Nationalist Chinese and Chiang Kai-Shek saw Chennault as a savior, while the war turned Chennault into a Major General, and a figure with an international reputation, especially in the Far East!

After the war, Chennault returned briefly to Louisiana (his home state) and a quiet retired life, but he almost immediately discovered that China was in his blood. Years of war had left China a war-ravaged cripple that had shattered her land, water, and air transportation system. Chennault returned to China to start an airline in which he undertook to move desperately needed relief supplies that had been sent by the United Nations Relief and Rehabilitation Administration—the UNRRA—but the supplies were on the docks and warehouses on the coast. In return for flying supplies into the interior of China where the supplies were needed, the new airline was given permission to fly commercial goods on the return flights instead of empty airplanes. The airline was called for a brief time UNRRA Air Transport. It was quickly changed to a simpler title, CAT—Civil Air Transport. That occurred on October 26, 1946, and a major airline was born.

CAT

After Chennault returned to China to start his airline he started looking for airplanes. He went to the Philippines, where he bought 20 Curtis C-46 Commandos and four Douglas C-47s that were all U.S. war surplus. They were all in Oahu in Hawaii. The first one arrived in Shanghai on March 2, 1947. They were almost all brand new, with less than 100 hours on the airframes, and a very good price. Also, the General bought 25 war-weary Curtis C-46s that were at Clark AFB, Philippines, and then flew them to China for spare parts for the new ones. Most of these newer airplanes stayed with the airline for many years through the end of the Vietnam War. This was financed by an agreement with former Flying Tiger pilot Robert Prescott, who, by now, was running his own air freight airline called, what else, Flying Tiger Airlines. Chennault was the heart and soul of CAT. He made it work and held it together.

The flights were originally all cargo, but as the Red Chinese rolled South in the late 1940s, creating some dangerous flying conditions (all aircraft were not Red Chinese, so they shot at *all* aircraft), CAT was carrying more and more human cargo. Whole orphanages were airlifted to safety, and a world's record evacuation of 7,000 people was made from the imperiled town of Mukden, China. Suddenly, CAT was in the passenger-carrying business, whether they liked it or not. But it still carried cargo and laid the pattern for the Berlin Airlift by supplying a major city—Taiyian, China, with a population of about 2,500,000—completely by air for the first time in history.

The interior Chinese airfields that they operated out of were mostly dirt strips or abandoned World War II fields. The CAT pilots were of the same breed as the original Flying Tigers—adventurers, individualists, and pilots who stayed in the Orient after the war.

CAT expanded rapidly, setting up more than 50 stations all over the vast regions of China. Business was very good. Some pilots were flying 18 hours a day. Pilot Randell Richardson flew 21 hours and 45 minutes on March 3, 1949 in one 24 hour day. Also, his aircraft picked up lots of bullet holes.

The airline was very successful at first, but CAT ran into increasing difficulties as the communists spread their control of mainland China, cutting off the routes of trade as they took over city after city. CAT met all requirements for international cargo airlift and was the Chinese flag passenger airline.

Early CAT operations had the makings of one of the most colorful, romantic, and in some respects, mysterious airlines in the history of aviation. General Claire Chennault once called CAT "the worlds' most shot-at airline."

Intermingled on these flights were agents of the newly formed Central Intelligence Agency, which was created in 1947 from the old O.S.S.—the Office of Strategic Services—that had been so successful in World War II. The nationalist Chinese were now losing the war against the Communists, and Mao Tse Sung and CAT began airlifting war material and ammunition into besieged cities. The CIA wanted to secretly airlift arms to anti-Communist Chinese groups using the only available transportation—CAT. But it was too little, too late. Since mainland China was economically falling apart, the revenues dropped off dramatically for CAT, and the Chinese money became almost worthless. CAT was about ready to go under when North Korea invaded South Korea on June 25, 1950. The CIA was quick to realize the excellent potential of owning their own airline, especially one that was already in place, very well known, and familiar in the region. Although CAT continued to act as a privately owned commercial airline, it began secretly to provide aircraft and crews for covert intelligence operations. As all of mainland China was taken over by the Red Chinese, CAT moved all of its operations, equipment, and offices to Formosa, or Taiwan as it is now known, along with the rest of the escaping Nationalist Chinese.

CAT was in desperate need of funds to continue to operate, so Chennault mentioned this to some of the CIA officials. A lawyer for CAT organized a new company called Civil Air Transport, Inc., allowing it to keep its original initials—CAT. The company was partially funded through the American Airdale Corporation, which was incorporated on July 10, 1950. Under this agreement, CAT was reorganized as a Delaware corporation under a CIA proprietary holding company. The Korean War had just started a few weeks earlier, and American interest had again turned toward the Far East.

When the war broke out, CAT's airlift capability suddenly became very sought after. During the first dangerous months of the Korean conflict, CAT pilots hauled 30% of all airlifted supplies into Korea.

The Korean War was to keep CAT flying at full speed for years, as the airlift capacity was in great demand for war supplies and material. At the time, CAT set up Korean Airlines as an adjunct operation. They are now a major airline of the world. The actual ownership of CAT was a closely held secret, and very classified. CAT continued to fly commercial routes throughout Asia, acting in every way as a privately-owned commercial airline. At the same time, the CIA provided airplanes and crews for secret intelligence operations in the Orient. CAT established the premier maintenance facilities of Asia at this time in Tainan, Formosa, and it was later used extensively by the U.S. Air Force for depot overhaul.

One war was to follow another for CAT; as the Korean War drew to a close, the French were heavily engaged in a losing battle in French Indochina. America wanted to assist the French, but indirectly. Therefore, CAT pilots flew many missions and supplies in Fairchild C-119s to Dien Bien Phu, and other locations in the area. To resupply Dien Bein Phu, CAT provided 24 pilots. Twelve C-119s were obtained from USAF stocks, with all USAF markings removed. The French roundel was added. No U.S. military personnel were involved. CAT flew 682 missions. Almost all of the C-119s were flak-damaged, and one was lost, piloted by James "Eathquake McGoon" McGovern, the legend of CAT and the Far East! Thus, this CAT operation brought about the first unofficial U.S.

casualty of the Vietnam War. These C-119s were serviced in Vietnam by the 81st Air Service Unit. By now, CAT had become the largest regional commercial airline in the Far East.

On October 7, 1957, the American Airdale Corporation changed its name to the Pacific Corporation in a reorganization to further hide the CIA's involvement in the airline. The Pacific Corporation became a holding company for Air Asia Company, Ltd., Air America, Inc., Civil Air Transport (CAT), Inc., Southern Air Transport, which operated in the Caribbean and South American areas, Intermountain Aviation, Bird and Sons (known as Bird Air), Robinson Brothers, plus others that came and went occasionally. Also, certain existing American airlines cooperated readily. Continental Airlines set up a subsidiary called Continental Air Service, Inc., or CASI, for operations and airlift support in Asia. Continental Airlines paid more than a million dollars in cash for the twenty-two aircraft and 350 employees of Bird Air, which became CASI. Continental Airlines still operates in the Pacific islands.

The Pacific Corporation was constantly leasing aircraft to one another, changing engines, tail numbers, and common parts supplies. This is not to suggest that the Pacific Corporation was a badly managed or ineffective corporation. It was a superbly run organization that made profits, had a great safety record, and did whatever job that it was asked to do, living up to the company slogan, "Anything, Anywhere, Anytime—Professionally."

CAT had two fatal accidents. The first one was on June 20, 1964, near Taiching, in central Taiwan. It was a highly suspicious crash of a CAT Curtis C-46, registered B-908. It was a domestic airliner flight that claimed the lives of 57 people, including the richest man in Asia at that time—Data Loke Wan Tho.

AIR AMERICA

The demise of CAT began with the death of Chennault in 1958. The name CAT was changed to Air America on March 31, 1959, as a further airline that owned another airline to conceal its actual ownership in another reorganization. Most of the aircraft were repainted from CAT to Air America, although numerous aircraft did not have any markings on them except for the registration numbers. CAT even still operated a few in a variety of markings. Some aircraft kept the CAT name and markings on them for years afterward. CAT even ordered a Convair 880 jet airliner for its Mandran Jet routes. It was later traded in for the Boeing 727. CAT and CAT, Inc., were two different companies owned by the Pacific Corporation. To avoid confusion, CAT, the established commercial airline, kept its name, and CAT, Inc., changed its name to Air America

The second and last accident that CAT had was fatal to the airline. The Boeing 727-027C, B-1018, crashed seven miles northwest of Taipei, killing 21 people, including some of the flight crew. The pilot killed was Hugh Hicks. His wife was onboard, and was also one of the fatalities. In the cockpit, also, was Stuart "Stu" Dew. Stu's arm arm was all but torn off. He was one of the original CAT pilots, and had been the personal pilot for General George C. Marshall, America's top military man (later Secretary of State) and author ofthe Marshall Plan that saved Europe in the late 1940s from Russian take-over. The crash on February 16, 1968, was basically the end of CAT. The airline had an astonishing record of accident-free flights, but the Chinese authorities in Taiwan were anxious to get rid of CAT. The accident gave the Chinese an excuse to cancel the airline's charter, and they replaced it with China Airlines, a wholly-owned Chinese operation.

CAT's headquarters were in Taipei, Formosa. They owned 99% of Air Asia, who operated one of the largest major maintenance facilities in the world at Tainen, Taiwan. By 1966, that complex would grow to have 5,000 employees and a net worth of over $22 million.

Flight equipment was modernized in the late 1950s and improved by adding Douglas DC-4s, Douglas DC-6s, and the Convair 880. Other specialized equipment was added as needed.

Air America's headquarters were at Udorn, Thailand, for Southeast Asia (Laos). Large operations and support worked very well. Udorn had a restaurant, movie theater, American school, bar, hand ball court, food store with liquor, and a swimming pool.

The outer ramp at Uborn had hard stands, tie downs, drainage, etc., for excellent support of operations. Shown here are three Sikorski UH-34s, Porter PC-6C, Beech Volpar, Bell 205, two more UH-34s, Fairchild C-123, and a CH-47. The small building is the Air America fire house.

On August 23, 1959, the first two transports of Air America arrived in Vientiane, Laos, and thus began a 15 year relationship with the area. On December 4, 1960, the first Soviet transport arrived in Vientiane, showing Russian interest in the area. Late in that month, an Air America transport was actually fired upon by a Soviet Ilyushin 14. This brought about a heightened tension of the Cold War that was turning hot in the Southeast Asia area. After 1960, Air America operations mushroomed when the CIA became involved in Laos. Due to the very rugged terrain in Laos, Air America bought its first new aircraft type. The Helio Courier was chosen, and they bought about a dozen of them for their operations in Laos. It immediately became the favorite workhorse, and operated for many years. The check out program in a Helio was very extensive. Frequently, the Helio was flown overloaded. The

accident rate was high due to this. It was a tricky airplane to operate. It had some very unusual characteristics, including the fact that it would ground-loop at the drop of a hat.

It was largely succeeded by the Pilatus PC-6 Porter, designed and built by Swiss engineers for operations in the Alps and on glaciers. Although the weather was distinctly different, the type of operations were very similar. The Porter was an old man's airplane compared to the Helio. It was an easier plane to fly, carried a bigger load, and could go into shorter strips more comfortably because of the reverse prop. In a Porter you could come in at 50 knots, easily touch down, come into reverse prop, and stop within 200 feet. The only Porter shortcoming was that it was not nearly as strong as the Helio. The survivability in a Porter was not nearly as good if you had to go into the jungle.

The inner ramp adjacent to the hangars and maintenance shops at Udorn were very functional. In the background are supply warehouses. A close look reveals a Beech Turbo Volpar, three Sikoski UH-34s (9349 is from the Royal Lao Air Force), a Porter PC-6C, and a Hughes OH-6A.

An American registered Beech Twin Bonanza, N9316Y, is in front of a LAO hangar in Vientene, Laos. Also in the background are a Continental Air Services, Inc. (CASI) C-40, a U.S. Army Beech U21A, a Beech Baron, and a Cessna.

Also added into the Air America stable was the Dornier Do-28, which was a German built aircraft used for larger loads and a more conventional landing strip, although the Dornier also had very good STOL performance. It also had twin-engine safety.

The de Havilland of Canada Caribou was probably the best airplane of the whole STOL fleet, because it was a comfortable twin-engined transport, and yet could get into many of the short strips, and it was a good STOL airplane. It could also carry a large load of cargo or personnel. In the Caribou, a typical day was a good solid eight hours of flying with twelve to 14 segments.

Air America was a very well run organization with an excellent Board of Directors. Air America was a well-organized, effective air carrier able to meet any national requirements with skilled crews ready to carry out any missions required of them. This was put to the test when the military activities that developed in Laos needed air support. Ground transportation was non-existent in Laos. Air America, using both fixed-wing and rotary-wing aircraft, was assigned some of the most demanding and dangerous flying. The role of Air America in the supply and movement of personnel and refugees, as well as the clandestine missions and the search-and-rescue operations, was a vital part of the overall U.S. effort in Southeast Asia in the 1960s and 1970s.

On July 23, 1962, the Protocol to the Declaration on the Neutrality of Laos was signed in Geneva, easing a critical superpower confrontation in Laos between Russia and the United States. The United States reduced its military presence in Laos to conform with the requirements of the Geneva Convention, but the North Vietnamese continued secretly to build up and strengthen their forces while enlarging the Ho Chi Minh trail that ran south through Laos towards South Vietnam. The North Vietnamese responded to the Lao Prime Minister Souvanna Phouma's repeated accusations and complaints by simply denying everything. This was shades of things to come ten years later during the negotiations in Paris with the Americans on ending the Vietnam War. To counter these North Vietnamese moves without provoking confrontation with the Soviet Union or China, President Kennedy and his advisors decided to continue support of a deniable, clandestine, largely paramilitary force within Laos with strict instructions that the actual fighting should be done by indigenous troops. This was done mainly with the Hmong mountain natives of Laos. They have always been called Hmong, which means "free men." A Hmong tribesman was unlikely to serve as a full-time soldier away from home unless he knew his family would be cared for in his absence, so a mutual relationship developed between General Yang Pao's army of Hmongs and Air America, which supported them.

Because no U.S. military planes were permitted to be based inside Laos, Air America came to play the essential role with its helicopters, transports, and STOL aircraft. Throughout this period, Thai leaders cooperated fully in the belief that it was better for the communist threat to be fought in Laos rather than on Thai soil.

Air America also became involved in Project Mill Pond in 1961 involving Douglas B-26s and Lockheed C-130s, and later on Project Black Watch. Operation Mill Pond was supervised by U.S. Air Force Major Harry C. "Heinie" Aderholt.

A Cessna U-17B and a North American T-28 are being jig rebuilt at Udorn by Air America. Air America provided maintenance support for other operators in the area, also.

The Air America flight line at Tan Son Nhut AFB, South Vietnam, in March of 1970 shows Caribou N539Y, Douglas C-47 083, and a Curtis C-46. (Bob Livingstone)

Major Aderholt was the commander of the 1095th Operational Evaluation Training Group, an Air Force organization that specialized in "cooperative efforts" with the CIA. At the same time Aderholt was also controlling C-46 airlift operations in Laos and coordinating (with the CIA and Air America) the surveying and establishment of small landing strips known as "Lima Sites." The Lima Sites, scattered throughout Laos, would soon become essential to Air America's effort in airborne resupply and personnel movement.

The landing site numbers used were based on the Air America system of identifying airfields and airstrips in Southeast Asia by a number with a prefix to indicate the country. Some sites had names so similar in spelling and pronunciation, especially in Laos, that a number system was necessary to avoid mass confusion. In Laos, additional letter prefixes differentiated small STOL strips and helicopter pads from the larger airfields. Larger airfield numbers were prefixed by an "L" for Laos. The smaller airstrips and helicopter pad numbers were prefixed by "LS" for Laos Site, or, as the pilots referred to them, Lima Sites (for example, Lima 213 or Lima Site 213, or simply Site 213, was Pha Hong). In Thailand, Cambodia, and Vietnam, all airfields, regardless of size, were identified by Tango "T," Charlie "C," and Victor "V," respectively.

Air America had four Sikorsky H-19s, but they needed more helicopters for their operations. So, in 1961, they were augmented by U.S. Marine Corps helicopter pilots, who volunteered to fly H-34s from a carrier in the Gulf of Siam, overfly Thailand, and land in Vientiane, Laos. Title to the helicopters passed to Air America. The Marines, through a process called "sheep dipping," were signed on as civilian employees of Air America. This was authorized by President Kennedy himself. Over the years, Air America obtained more ex-Marine H-34s. Some were converted to turbine power at the Tainen maintenance facilities. Many were stationed at Udorn AFB, Thailand. Air America thereby established its Thailand

A Bell 205 (UH-ID) is undergoing a major overhaul at Udorn, Thailand. It is painted Navy blue and natural metal. In the background is a Sikorski S-58T, XW-PHD, the turbine-powered version of the UH-34.

A Beech Volpar undergoes a major landing gear repair, and a 100-hour inspection. The Volpar maintenance was carried out at Air Asia, Ltd., facilities in Tainan, Taiwan.

Beech Volpar, N3728G, at Vientene, Laos, is in front of a hangar and training building. 28G was one of the aerial photographic aircraft.

operations, building a base that was to become the corner-stone of Air America's operation in Laos. This policy would characterize their activities in Laos for many years to come—extensive CIA paramilitary operations by Thailand-based Air America. Since the U.S. government insisted that no U.S. military aircraft were allowed to be based inside supposedly neutral Laos, Air America played an essential role. The Geneva Accords signed on July 23, 1962, prohibited foreign military personnel from being stationed in Laos.

Air America was the only air-rescue system in the area during the early 1960s. Air America helicopter crews have never been given any recognition for their bravery in picking up downed airmen in Laos, something that they were not obligated to do. Since they were shot at frequently during their air rescue missions, Royal Laotian Air Force North American T-28s were used for their escort and cover for the Air America helicopters. The T-28s were not allowed to shoot unless the Air America helicopters were shot at. Some of the T-28s had RLAF markings, but most were just plain generic aircraft. On November 27, 1962, a Pathet Lao antiaircraft gun emplacement shot down an Air America Curtis C-46 Commando.

On December 6, 1963, CINCPAC (Commander in Chief, Pacific—usually a 4-star Admiral) recommended to the Sec-

retary of Defense that a T-28 Commando detachment from the USAF Special Air Warfare Center at Eglin AFB, Florida, be deployed to Udorn, Thailand, to protect these Air America helicopters, and to further train the Laotian T-28 pilots. In March of 1964, 38 U.S. Air Force men of Detachment 6, 1st Air Commando Wing, code name "Operation Waterpump," arrived at Udorn AFB, Thailand. Detachment 6 later became part of the 606th Air Commando Squadron in 1966, and then the 56th Air Commando Wing in 1967. Using Air America equipment at Udorn, the detachment established a T-28 main-tenance facility and began a T-28 flight school for Thai and Laotian pilots. As graduates of this training became opera-tional and more functional, there were fewer calls for Air America T-28 pilots flying the Laotian T-28s. The pilots were already well qualified flyers. CIA and Air America officials in Vientiane quickly and secretly recruited more Air America ci-vilian pilots to fly along with the T-28s. On May 20, 1964, the State Department authorized Air America to fly the T-28s on offensive missions. Since this was "out of the scope" of air-line operations, something different was arranged. The Ameri-can ambassador to Laos advised Prime Minister Souvanna to issue papers to these pilots and to "terminate" their em-ployment with Air America so that the pilots would have sta-tus of civilian technicians hired by the Royal Laotian Air Force

UH-34s are being recon-structed from the remains of other Sikorskis. The jigs were locally manufactured. Heavy maintenance was done at Udorn, Thailand, while depot maintenance (if possible) was done at Tainen. (Ward Reimer)

The Air America Chalet, or terminal, at Sam Thong, Laos, was a typical larger base stop for Air America. Sam Thong was called LS-20, or landing sight 20, or Lima Site 20.

Another typical airstrip for Air America customers was Ban Jeng Drom in Laos as shown in June of 1964.

until Thai and Laotian pilots were fully qualified to support the Air America rescue efforts.

As the support of ground operations of General Vang Pao increased, the need for directing airstrikes evolved. The "Butterflies" were Forward Air Controllers (FACs) flying in the right seat of Air America or Continental Air Services, Inc. (CASI) aircraft, usually in the Helio Courier or the Porter. These men were also "sheepdipped" military personnel. They were issued a Laotian driver's license and wore civilian clothes, and were given papers identifying them as employees of a civilian agency in Laos. They directed airstrikes, not only for USAF and U.S. Navy aircraft, but also for Laotian, Hmong, and Thai pilots. The Butterfly FAC had a pilot next to him, and often a Laotian or Hmong interpreter sitting in back. They used standard USAF procedures so well that none of the pilots realized they were being controlled by "civilians." Later, 120 U.S. Air Force personnel were assigned to Thailand, but they were really "sheepdipped" FAC pilots called "Ravens." This was their call sign. They were volunteers with previous experi-

ence in one of the Tactical Air Control Squadrons in Vietnam. Initially assigned to Long Tieng and then to Luang Prabang, Vientene, and Savannakhet and Pakse, they usually flew Cessna O-1s. Maineneance was done by Air America on Raven O-ls and U-17s (Cessna 180s).

Since there were no reliable charts or navigation aids in Laos, some mapping and reconnaissance missions were undertaken by C-47s in late 1960 and early 1961, but the vulnerable C-47 was replaced with un-marked RT-33s in April of 1961. A number of aircraft were shot at and hit, but none were lost. Therefore, the USAF brought in some RF-101Cs under Project Able Mable. The could fly faster and higher and achieve the same results quicker.

On June 6, 1964, a U.S. Navy RF-8 Crusader from Yankee Station flown by Lt. Charles F. Klusmann was shot down by Communist gunfire while on a mission over the northeast corner of the Plain of Jars. Within an hour, Air America transport planes had located the pilot and called for a rescue pickup by Air America H-34s. As the helicopters descended, they

A typical landing site in the remote mountains of Laos shows a Pilatus PC-6 Porter on the end of the runway—if you can call it a runway.

Song Lai, Laos (landing sight 318, or LS-318) shows a PC-6 Porter, N391R, on the runway on March 21, 1972.

A Porter of Continental Air Services, Inc. (CASI), is in a typical valley somewhere in Laos. The Porter, XW-PDI, was one of the very few Laotian-registered Porters.

were hit by more gunfire. Four Thai piloted T-28s were sent from Vientiane to provide cover for the rescue. They could not find the rescue area, so American piloted T-28s were sent. By the time they arrived there, however, the Pathet Lao had captured Lt. Klusmann. The next day, while flying in the same area, another Navy aircraft was hit. The pilot ejected successfully and was picked up the following day by an Air America H-34.

The loss of two Navy reconnaissance aircraft resulted in immediate American action. Air America T-28s were now authorized to do all possible to protect the rescue helicopters. CINCPAC recommended that Air America be provided with at least five additional H-34s. This was a wise decision, and it paid off substantially in future rescue operations.

An Air America Helio Courier on a very remote landing sight in the Laotian mountains proves that there were no level runways in the hills.

On August 14, a T-28 was forced down and a F-105 was damaged. Four days later, another T-28 was shot down, along with an Air America H-34 responding for a rescue attempt. Fortunately, three Air America T-28s and a number of U.S. Air Force F-100s were able to provide cover fire while an Air America H-34 successfully rescued the American pilot.

Then, on November 21, 1964, a McDonnell RF-101C Voodoo on a reconnaissance mission was shot down 40 miles east of Thakhet. The pilot ejected and came down in the jungle. An Air America H-34 happened to be in the area and recovered the pilot within an hour. By this time, it was evident that the Air Force Air Rescue Service was not yet able to handle the rescue mission in Laos. So, shortly thereafter in 1965, the Air Force sent air-rescue units to Udorn and Nakhon Phanom, Thailand.

Heavy anti-aircraft weapons were brought into southern Laos in early 1966 by the Pathet Lao. It is estimated that there were up to 10,000 anti-aircraft guns in all of Laos by 1967, ranging in size from .51 caliber to 57 mm. Therefore, some USAF Douglas B-26Ks were deployed to take out some of these gun positions. These missions were classified as Project Big Eagle missions, which became a part of Project Lively Tiger. All of these missions were classified, and the aircraft had no markings.

Laos was divided up into three separate areas for air operations. The areas were called Steel Tiger, Tiger Hound, and Barrell Roll. Barrell Roll was basically northern Laos and the Plain of Jars, which was called PDJ. The initials in French meant Plaine De Jars. The jars on the plain were large crock pots holding human remains. They were grouped to form cemeteries, and they were great navigational aids. PDJ, a

Douglas C-54D-115-DC, serial 10869, was originally built as 42-72764. After World War II, when it was stationed in the Pacific area, it was purchased by CAT, which later became Air America. These aircraft were stripped so light that they could carry 22,000 pounds of cargo and 10 hours of fuel. There were no toilets, no heat, no amenities at all. (Robert Mikesh)

high rolling grassland located in the center of northern Laos, is surrounded by some of the highest mountains in Southeast Asia. Also, the area has historically been an important crossroads for commerce moving between Vietnam and the Mekong river valley.

Rice dropping was one of the main functions of Air America. They did a lot of rice drops, both hard and soft (hard rice was ammunition and weapons). They would triple sack about 80 pounds of rice placed in an inner 200 pound or 100 kilo bag, so it was very loose. If you dropped it from about

800 feet, by the time it hit the ground, it had lost all of its forward momentum. Sometimes it would rupture the first or second sack, but rarely the third one. Air America crews became very adept at delivering air drops of supplies.

For an example of the depth of aircraft ownership that Air America had on some of its aircraft, let us look at the Douglas B-26, N46598, nick-named "Blue Goose." It was listed as an On-Mark conversion, but, in fact, it was more than that. It was originally built as a A-26B-55-DL, serial 44-34415, the 818th A-26 built. This B-26 (as the A-26s were now known)

After service with CAT and later Air America, the registration remained the same—B1014. As shown here in March of 1969 at Danang AFB, South Vietnam, it had almost no markings at all. (Robert Mikesh)

B-910 was a Curtis C-46A that was at Danang AFB, South Vietnam, in April of 1968. Air America had dozens of Curtis C-46 Commandos. (Robert Mikesh)

in 1966, ownership of the B-26 was in the hands of Pan Aero Investment Corporation of Reno, Nevada, when it was sold to Air America in April of 1967. It was re-registered at that time as N46598. It was operating in Laos by this time.

In March of 1968, it was transferred to Overseas Aeromarine, Inc., of Seattle, Washington. Overseas Aeromarine then notified the FAA on April 30, 1968, that the aircraft was scrapped. But reports later were that it was still operating out of Udorn, Thailand. The crew who flew it called it the "Blue Goose," or "Blivit." It was camouflaged a dark blue color for nighttime operations. The engines were R-2800CB16/17s with water injection. The windshield was from a Douglas DC-6 or DC-7. It also had a DC-6 or DC-7 landing gear and fuselage, including windows. The cabin floor had rollers or tracks to take cargo loaded on pallets (not necessarily rice), which could be dropped over a ramp out the rear of the plane. Some of these modifications had been done at Air Asia in Tainen.

Operating in an area where growing crops from which various illegal drugs were developed and the production of these various farms of illegal drugs is endemic to the local economies, it was inevitable that rumors would be heard, that the airline or its employees were involved in the illegal trade. It was an easy propaganda line to be developed by unfriendly interests. Air America management had foreseen the danger and took every possible step to make sure that there would be no truth to such stories. In fact, at Udorn, Air America had a narcotics inspection group consisting of 15 personnel who performed detailed inspections, using trained dogs, of aircraft and personnel entering and leaving the facility.

Air America's role in Vietnam was visible as it was secret in Laos. The airline was everywhere in Vietnam where most of its operations were above board. Air America, by 1966, had almost 6,000 employees. At its peak in 1970, Air America was, in terms of the numbers of aircraft owned or had avail-

went to an Asian classified project on October 13, 1960, from the storage facilities at Davis-Monthan AFB near Tuscon, Arizona. On July 12, 1962, it was re-registered as N5002X, with ownership with Intermountain Aviation in Phoenix, Arizona, a company owned by the Pacific Corporation. Quite a few other aircraft were re-registered in sequence (N5001X, 02X, 03X, etc.) at this time. Intermountain sold the B-26 to On-Mark Engineering in July, 1963. Early in 1964, the conversions had been completed, and it was sold back to Intermountain. It was then passed over to LTV Temco Aerosystems Division in Greenville, Texas, for installations of volumes of electronics, including terrain-following radar, used then on the new F-111s. This was completed by November of 1964. At this time, the ownership passed to Atlantic General Enterprises, Inc., of Washington, D.C., probably another CIA company. It was then sold back to Intermountain Aviation. Early

Curtis C-46D, B-928, was one of about 40 Curtis C-46s that was operated by Air America at various times. This photo was taken in March of 1968 at Danang. (Robert Mikesh)

B-928 was a Chinese-registered Commando that was visiting Danang AFB, South Vietnam. (Robert Mikesh)

able, the largest airline fleet in the world, although a lot of aircraft were small, a lot were helicopters, and the total number was unknown, even to the agency. By comparisons, its "competitor," the Flying Tiger Line, which was the largest all-cargo airline in the world at that time, had 22 aircraft, and about 2,100 employees, in 1968.

The CIA was known as "the customer," ammunition became "hard rice," and any secret mission was classified as "black." Personnel dropped in enemy territory (Indian country) were called "infils" and "exfils" when they were brought out. Good guys were called "friendlies," and the enemy was called "bad guys."

Probably the biggest part of the Air America mission was support of refugee supply, movement, and resettlement. Air America could supply enough food and supplies in a single morning to supply and feed 5,000 people for a month. Of

course, there is no question that they were also very active in the military end of it, in trying to supply General Yang Pao and his military personnel in various locations around Laos. Another part of the Air America mission was to monitor the "McNamara Fence," which was code named Igloo White. That was a strip of land along the 17th parallel that separated North and South Vietnam and extended across the Ho Chi Minh trail into Laos. It was strewn with remote sensors monitored by aircraft. It was a multi-billion dollar effort that did not work. Air America operated the Volpars over the McNamara Fence for monitoring the fence. The Volpars were turbo-prop conversions of a twin Beechcraft model 18.

There were also special projects that were for volunteers only. The only thing that was done on some of these missions was resupplying teams or listening outposts. They traveled light and needed to be resupplied frequently. The only

C-46D-20-CU, serial 22228, was originally built as 44-78405. Chinese registered as B-858, this Air America Commando was visiting K-8 (Kunsan), Korea, in February of 1964. (Robert Mikesh)

Curtis C-46, B870, visits Tachikawa AFB, Japan, in May of 1957 on a cargo mission. Although belonging to CAT, it carried no markings. All CAT, and later Air America, C-46s were bare metal. However, there was one C-46 with a light blue color scheme on it. (Robert Mikesh)

way to do that safely was at night. They would send a radio message giving a location. There would be an agreed upon pattern for a strobe and light signal that pilots would look for when they got to the area. The signals had to match, or there was no drop. Sometimes there was no voice communication, and sometimes there was. There were other volunteer, or black missions, also. Pilots and crew would disappear for eight or ten days (on leave?) at a time.

Headquarters for the Pacific Corporation was in Washington, D.C. Flying operations were based in Vientiane, Laos, Saigon, Vietnam, Clark AFB, Philippines, Udorn AFB, Thailand, Yokota AFB, Japan, Kadina AFB, Okinawa, and Hong Kong, China. Also, Air Asia, Ltd., had its headquarters in Taipei, Taiwan, and its huge maintenance facilities in Tainan, Taiwan.

At Udorn AFB, Thaland, Air America even had a dependents school for employees' children and families. Also at Udorn was where operations, technical support, and maintenance was done for most Air America flight equipment.

The average Air America pilot was not a mercenary pilot, but had about 10,000 flight hours, and several had over 15,000 hours. Air America operated from 28,000 to 30,000 flights per month by 1970. They were not war-loving redneck adventurers. To put their lives on the line, as they did, required more than just a desire for money and adventure. They differed from purely mercenary soldiers of fortune in that they would not have sold their skills to just any country for money. They liked the money, but the accompanying psychological income was important—the feeling that they were doing it for America, the personal satisfaction of challenging the terrain, weather, and the enemy by flying by the seat of their pants in prop airplanes! Also, the feeling that they were supporting a brave people in the defense of their homeland. The flying was very interesting and challenging to the pilots. They were flying in

an area which was, even without an enemy shooting at you, very hostile. There were no navigational aids to speak of.

The average flight was only about 20 minutes—some pilots flew 68 missions in one day in fixed-wing aircraft. All fixed-wing aircraft checked in with flight operations every 30 minutes for security and safety. The entire flyable fleet was usually committed every day to flight operations.

During the war, Air America flew throughout South Vietnam, Thailand, and Cambodia, but their main operations were in Laos. In northern Laos, strips that were suitable for de Havilland Caribous were 4,500 feet in elevation, 1300 feet long, and 50 feet wide. None were level. Air America flew into a lot of high altitude (over 6,000 feet) airfields. Most airfields had tricky wind currents, and were very challenging and difficult to conduct operations from. Air America provided air support for American objectives in Laos, mainly through USAID.

B-870 was C-46D-20-CU, serial number 2232, and was built as 44-78409. It is shown here at Tachikawa AFB, Japan, in May of 1957. It was being operated by CAT at the time. (Robert Mikesh)

Curtis C-46D-20-CU, serial 22228, was built as 44-78404, where it first flew on May 29, 1945. It was sold to CAT, which became Air America. B-858 is shown here at Kusan (K-8), Korea. It was one of the original low-time C-46s purchased for CAT in 1946. (Robert Mikesh)

They supplied the approximately 45,000-man army of General Vang Pao. Air America's main objective was logistical.

Air America tried to use as many local nationals as possible. This raised their local skill levels and standard of living to levels that otherwise would not have been possible, and, thus, Air America gained the support of the local people. Air America hired more Laotian people than any other company. Most missions were to Laotian villages (whose only contact to the outside world was Air America) with food, medicine, etc. Most Laotians lived on mountain peaks where it was cool. Down in the valleys there was heat, mosquitos, jungle, floodings, and Pathet Lao. One Laotian village chief was so fascinated by the rice drops that he asked if he could go up in an Air America airplane to see where rice came from.

Laotian landing strips were just planed-off mountain ridge lines with high elevations, and were only about 400 to 600 feet long. Most had a 15 or 20 degree bend on them. Most were about 35 feet wide. Upslopes were usually 5 to 30 degrees. Wind gusts were most dangerous in the mountains, and thermals were everywhere. Most fields had a great deal of ruts, erosion, and washouts. The weather changed very rapidly, and Laos had very rugged terrain. There were no weather reporting stations in northern Laos. Laos has five months of intensive rains, and seven months of summer heat. It is a remote, under-developed country—a very demanding environment.

In Vietnam, Air America served 12,000 passengers monthly. There were USAID people, missionaries, military

B-858 was a frequent visitor to Korea. It was later registered as XW-PFL. Its fate is unknown. (Robert Mikesh)

Curtis C-46D-20-CU, serial 32985, was built as 44-77589, and later it was registered as N9458Z. It was actually owned by Southern Air Transport. It survived the war with over 20,000 hours, and was sold to Oasis in the Philippines as RP-C1442. It is being serviced at Danang AFB, South Vietnam, in March of 1968 as shown in this photograph. The Curtis C-46 was designed for a service life of 50,000 hours. (Robert Mikesh)

personnel, correspondents, government officials, nurses, etc. Air America also did psy-ops in support of USAF operations. From 38 to 40 Air America aircraft were based in Vietnam at its peak.

Lots of "black" operations were done out of Takhli, including Douglas DC-4s and Boeing 727s. Parachuting out the rear door of a 727 was developed by Air America long before D.B. Cooper completed the first and only successful hijacking in history in 1971 of a Northwest Airlines Boeing 727 over the state of Washington. The aircraft involved would fly to Takhli, be sterilized (removal of national insignias, names, serial numbers, etc.), fly the mission, return to Takhli, and the markings would be re-installed. This happened so frequently that some aircraft had brackets holding on the marking that would just be slipped out for the mission. These type of missions frequently occurred on weekends, since they were being utilized during the week on other scheduled flights. These type of missions were the exception, though.

Frequently, when a very sensitive mission was required and no United States military personnel were allowed to participate, Air America was called upon to fly the mission. The mission might require a specific type of aircraft not in the Air America fleet, so that type of aircraft was "loaned" to Air America, all military markings were removed, and the Air America crew was trained or checked-out. This is another reason that Air America crews were so proficient and highly skilled. Once the mission was completed, the aircraft was returned to the military. Thus, Air America operated various other types of aircraft, but were usually on a "one time" basis. This book covers only the main operational daily-use of aircraft utilized by Air America, and not the "one time" equipment. One type of this sort of support mission was the RWT, or "road watch teams." These were in support of personnel

monitoring the Ho Chi Minh trail in Laos. Usually, CH-3 and later CH-53 helicopters were used. These missions were called Pony Express missions.

At the Udorn facilities of Air America there were simulators. Each Air America pilot was required to have 8 hours of "sim" time annually, and two check rides annually.

Air Asia Ltd. did heavy maintenance on large aircraft—overhaul, repair, and depot level maintenance on many types of aircraft and engines. The average was about 75 aircraft in maintenance at one given time, including F-4s, F-100s, F-105s, and all Air America flight equipment. They had about

Curtis C-46, B-985, displays its beautiful Air America markings in Okinawa in the mid-1960s, where it flew an airline schedule. This C-46 had Hamilton Standard propellors, which are very rare on C-46s. Also, prop spinners were rarely used, but are on this C-46F-1-CO, which was delivered to the USAAF as 44-78715. This is the only known C-46 in this Air America color scheme. The rest of the fleet was bare metal.

C-46, B-924, shows the cockpit area on October 31, 1966. Visibility from the cockpit of the C-46 was very good. (Tom Hansen)

The small cargo loading door was on the right side of the Curtis C-46. The horizontal tubes above the door are reinforcement strips. The large cargo loading door is on the left side of the aircraft. (Tom Hansen)

4,000 employees—99% were Chinese, and most were very well educated and skilled. Heavy checks were done at Tainan, and they did training, work instructions, manuals, and parts support. They had approximately 120,000 line items. They also had a Douglas B-26 for training.

At Kadena AFB on Okinawa, Air America had 225 operations per month, even though they started operations only in 1954. However, All Nippon Airways took over this service in 1967.

Flying slow, unarmed, vulnerable aircraft over dangerous, hostile territory can be very hazardous. Many Air America aircraft were shot down and lost. The first one was a Curtis C-46 that was shot down on November 27, 1962, over the Plain of Jars. Air America lost 242 men during its lifespan.

In 1966, the U.S. Air Force established a very secret navigation (TACAN) sight in northern Laos. Designated Lima Site 85 (LS 85), it could be reached only by Helio Couriers or helicopters. On January 12, 1968, LS 85 was attacked by three North Vietnamese Soviet-built Antonov An-2 Colt aircraft with no markings, and equipped with machine guns fired from the windows and hand thrown grenades. In one of the most bizarre air engagements ever, an Air America helicopter crew flying a Bell UH-1B (model 204) chased and engaged the three attacking NVAF aircraft, and shot down one of the An-2s with a confiscated carbine! The second An-2 was forced down and crashed into a mountain, and the third was chased for 18 miles by the Air America crew until it, too, was forced down through superior airmanship!

By the early 1970s, the war in Vietnam was winding down, and, therefore, so were Air America operations. Also, the CIA had changed its policy about airplanes and airlines. The days of wholly-owned agency proprietaries seemed to be over. They proved finally to be unwieldy, vulnerable to media exposure, and no longer necessary. It was no longer confidential, and was one of the widest "known" secrets in the world, that the

CIA owned Air America. Therefore, the Pacific Corporation decided to slowly dissolve itself. By this time, the secret war in Laos had became public knowledge, and the anti-Vietnam war sentiment obscured the story of Hmong sacrifices in defense of their homelands, in helping American efforts to stem the tide of war materials flowing down the Ho Chi Mihn trail, and in rescuing American pilots and crew members shot down over the jungles of Laos. General Vang Pao, who headed the Hmong war effort, was assumed by some to be a warlord who profited from the opium trade, but this simply was not true.

Air America sold Southern Air Transport on December 31, 1971, and it still operates out of Miami, Florida, to this day. Also, Air America sold its Intermountain Aviation company to Evergreen Helicopters. They still exist in Oregon. Air Asia, Ltd., the enormous repair and maintenance facilities (the largest in the Pacific), generated over $1 million worth of

Two Pratt & Whitney 2,000 HP R-2800s powered the Curtis C-46, and they were very adequate, as shown here at Danang AFB, South Vietnam, in October of 1966. (Tom Hansen)

A Curtis C-46 lands with its cargo at Danang AFB, South Vietnam, in May of 1966. Most C-46 loads were in the 12,000 to 15,000 pound range.

business per month in 1970. It was sold in 1975. At the time, Air Asia, Ltd.'s main facilities had over 360,000 square feet of ramp space, and 150,000 square feet of hangar space. They could accommodate any existing type of military or commercial jet. Also, Air Asia had 216,000 square feet of fully equipped and staffed shop facilities manned by 2,000 experienced personnel, engine test stands, 44,000 square feet of warehousing spare parts, 67,000 square feet of storage area, and 39,000 square feet of gas and chemical storage. Also, there were about 200 company vehicles, some water treatment

plants, and emergency diesel power plants. It was a huge facility!

On June 30, 1974, the Air America operations at Udorn, Thailand, closed down. These facilities were considered by the U.S. military to be one of he finest in Asia, and would have been perfect to maintain the Lao Air Force, but the Thai government opposed the presence in Thailand of the high-profile foreign military. The last flight was a Volpar mission to Bangkok and Saigon flown by Jim Rhyne. The gradual winding down of the U.S. presence in Indochina was mirrored by

Curtis C-46F-1-CU, B-146, taxies out for another mission from Danang AFB, South Vietnam, in September of 1966. It was originally built for the USAAF as 44-78638, serial 22461. (Tom Hansen)

Curtis C-46, B-924, returns to Danang AFB after another mission for a customer in September of 1966. (Tom Hansen)

a cutting back of Air America's total capacity. By 1975, the Pacific Corporation had trimmed the all-time high of 11,000 employees directly accountable to it in 1970 down to 1,100. Air America had been so strongly associated with the CIA that it was decided the best method of disposing of it was liquidation.

Operation Frequent Wind was the evacuation of Saigon as the North Vietnamese Army advanced toward the city in April of 1975. Air America responded to the call magnificently, and initiated the largest aerial evacuation in history. The unsung heroes of the airlift were the Air America Bell UH-1 Huey crews, who put in sterling work ferrying evacuees from around the city to either the U.S. embassy or the DAO compound. They were transporting personnel out to sea to awaiting aircraft carriers, refueling on the carriers, and returning to a disintegrating Saigon. From April 6, 1975, through April 30, 1975, a total of 51,888 people were flown out of Saigon. Of these,

45,125 (87%) were flown out by Air America. 7,014 were flown out on April 29 and 30 alone, with 5,595 (80%) evacuated by Air America. Several helicopters were lost during the evacuation due to enemy fire.

The CIA told the Senate Committee of Intelligence Operations that Air America would be phased out by June 30, 1976, ending its airlift capacity, and would sell assets and return millions of dollars to the U.S. Treasury.

Air America committed its men to a long line of losing battles. They were chased from the mainland of China, shot out of the sky while supporting the French at the besieged garrison of Dien Bien Phu, and were among the last to leave when Laos, Cambodia, and Vietnam collapsed. They were to receive no medals for these brave tasks, which were often too delicate, or simply too dangerous, for the military to undertake. Instead, tainted with the CIA by the liberal media and politians, their very existence had been denied by the

B-146, Curtis Commando, returns to Tan Son Nhut AFB, near Saigon, in September of 1966. A PC-6 Porter in the background is just leaving the Air America ramp. (Author)

Curtis C-46, B-146, turns into the Air America ramp at Tan Son Nhut AFB, South Vietnam, in September of 1966. The brakes on a C-46 were very squeeky, and one could always hear them coming as the brakes were applied. B-146 was originally delivered to the USAAF as 44-78638. (Author)

B-858, was a Chinese registered Curtis C-46D-20-CU operated by Air America in Vietnam. The Air America facilities at Tan Son Nhut AFB were next to the USAF C-123 flight line and MACV flight line. (Author)

Curtis C-46, B-910, is parked on the Air America flight line at Tan Son Nhut AFB, South Vietnam, in February of 1967. (Author)

government, while their fellow countrymen largely dismissed them as rednecks following a mercenary mission.

There would never be anything like Air America again. Its time had run out, and its usefullness was over. The unique mixture of extraordinary men of which it was made up had were now engaged in other endeavors.

Former Air America members are encouraged to contact the following:

Air America Association
P O Box 1522
Castroville, TX 78009-1522

There is a plaque on the main entrance wall of the Central Intelligence Agency in Langley, Virginia, honoring the 243 Air America men killed in action and missing in action. None are listed on the Vietnam Memorial Wall at Washington, D.C.,

although they also made the supreme sacrifice for their country during the Vietnam War era.

There is also a huge plaque that covers an entire wall listing all of the 243 men killed in action while operating with Air America. It is located at the University of Texas, Dallas, in the university library in Richardson, Texas, where Air America has a small archive.

Due to the highly classified nature of some of the Air America missions, and the general secretiveness of the CIA, photographs of, and the types of aircraft utilized by Air America are hard to come by. Cameras were prohibited on most missions. The photographs and data compiled in this story have not come from CIA sources or any other official U.S. Government sources, but mainly from private collections and other origins, some of which wish to remain anonymous. The Freedom of Information Act does not necessarily apply to the CIA.

Curtis C-46, B-148, returns to the Air America facilities at Tan Son Nhut AFB, South Vietnam, in September of 1966. In the background is an Air America de Havilland DHC-4A Caribou. (Author)

Curtis C-46F-1-CU, serial 22579, was registered as N67984, and originally built as 44-78756 for the USAAF. It was also operated by Flying Tigers Lines, Arctic Pacific Airlines, Pacific Western Airlines, and Air America. It is shown here at Tan Son Nhut AFB in February of 1970. This C-46 survived the war and was sold to Lancia Airlines as AN-BRC. (Bob Livingstone)

A Curtis C-46 of Air America leaves for another mission in February of 1967 from Tan Son Nhut AFB near Saigon, South Vietnam. (Author)

Continental Air Services, Inc. (CASI) was a close cousin to Air America, and also operated Curtis C-46s like N1447, serial 22561, which was originally built for the USAAF as 44-78738. It was still operating in 1973 when Laos was overrun.

The crew pushes out bags of rice on an airdrop resupply mission from a Curtis C-46. Note the rollers on the floor, and the crew who are wearing safety parachutes.

Curtis C-46A-45-CU, serial 30252, Laotian registered XW-PHM, was originally built as 42-96590, and delivered to the USAAF on July 10, 1944. It was operated by CASI in Laos. The color scheme was the standard Continental Airlines markings of that time. This C-46 did make it out of Laos in 1973, and survived the conflict is Southeast Asia. It was then sold to Amco Air.

Flying in Southeast Asia with Air America

I was in South East Asia for almost 18 years. Most of those years were flying Douglas DC-6 transport type aircraft from Japan, Korea, Okinawa, the Philippines, Vietnam, Thailand, and Laos. We, at CAT, Inc., and Air America, flew personnel and cargo throughout the area.

From time to time, emergency situations would develop in the area, and CAT, Inc., or Air America, crews and planes would be hastily dispatched from Udorn or Japan or where ever, to the trouble spot. In the late 1950s we usually flew out of Bangkok hauling cargo and supplies into various parts of Laos. It was a most exotic location, and flying into the remote parts of Laos was an "interesting" experience. While we did receive gunfire directed at our slow transports and helicop-

ters, we were usually fairly safe. Years later, the accuracy, size, and volume of the guns shooting at Air America increased, and so did the danger.

Navigational aids were almost non-existent in Laos. The weather tended to be wet-and-dry seasons with a few months of flying in which visibility was restricted by smoke. The mountain people traditionally used a slash-and-burn method of agriculture.

Laos was invaded by the North Vietnamese around 1960. The Hmong were willing to fight to defend their land, culture, and environment. The United States agreed to help. Air America was their airline, and their means of supply. We flew food (usually rice), and most anything else you could imagine that would fit into an airplane or a helicopter. Almost all

Curtis C-46D, XW-PBW, at a remote landing sight (LS) in Laos, picks up customers. This C-46 carries the Laotian insignia and flag of the Royal Lao Air Force, in addition to the civilian registration. Air America did maintenance support for the Laotian Air Force. This aircraft crashed on October 15, 1974, seventy-five miles north-east of Vientene, Laos

Curtis C-46, XW-PEJ, was one of about 20 Laotian registered C-46s. They were all bare metal and the markings were in black. All Laotian registered C-46s were based in Vientene. Laos.

airfields were remote landing sights. Other times, we air-dropped supplies into inaccessible areas. Sometimes we would be asked to fly large 155 mm howitzers. Other times, we would be asked to fly live animals and livestock. Our cargos were just about everything imaginable. And then there were the days we transported young Hmong soldiers to battle areas like to the Long Tieng battle around 1970.

As the years went by, the savagery of the war in Laos became more intense. There were fewer and fewer Hmong warriors left to fight the North Vietnamese and the Pathet Lao. Mostly they were just teenage boys. Most of the older men had been killed fighting the invaders. More and more Air America aircraft were being shot down. More and more Air America deaths were happening by gunfire.

But it was the most exciting time of my life. We really did a tremendous job over there. And we saved thousands of lives.

Jesse Walton
Air America pilot

Curtis C-46, XXW-PEJ, lands at Udorn, Thailand, after another mission. Notice the Caribou and the Helio U-10 in the background.

Curtis C-46 of Air America undergoing maintenance on the left Pratt & Whitney R-2800 engine at a remote airfield in the hilly Laotian countryside.

Special Delivery

I was ferrying a new Caribou to Vietnam. I was almost to Vietnam, uneventfully, when I contacted Cam Ranh Bay AFB approach about 50 miles offshore. They asked me if I could authenticate by giving the secret password of the day. I could not, since I was coming in from out of the country and I was not briefed on its need. Cam Rahn Bay AFB then scrambled the alert F-4s to come out and identify me. I was on the same frequency as the F-4s as they came to intercept me in my Caribou. They were test firing their guns (SUU-20 gun pods), and whatever else they do. My co-pilot, who was fairly new, just knew they were going to shoot us down! I knew they wouldn't, and tried to console him, but to no avail.

Suddenly, the two F-4s came screaming by from our 6 o'clock position and just above our cockpit. That *did* get our attention! We were doing about 110 knots, and they must have been doing about 400 knots. The lead F-4 asked his wingman, "Did you get his tail number?" The wingman replied, "No, he was too slow." The lead pilot said, "Well, let's go around and try it again." I had a great idea! I asked the new copilot for full flaps, and landing gear down. I was going to slow down to about 50 knots, and have some fun with the F-4s. An almost empty Caribou with full flaps and everything down will really fly slow! With a strong head wind, a Caribou will almost HOVER! My copilot begged me not to do it. He was still terrified they would shoot us down. The F-4s came back again. They had flaps and everything hanging to slow down, but they were still too fast. The same conversation then occurred between the F-4 pilots. I saw a small cumulus cloud ahead and decided to go into the cloud and orbit at 50 knots with full rudder. I am sure that I appeared to them to be hovering.

Beech 18, N137L, of Air America visits the Hue Citadel airfield in January of 1968, just before the battle for that city the following month. (Robert Mikesh)

Now they were really confused. I still had not said anything to the F-4s. Soon, one of the F-4s said, "We can't go until we get his tail number. I don't know what to do. Nothing in the book about this." To ease their predicament, I asked them if they wanted me to give them my tail number so they could go home. They said "Yes," and were ever so thankful! As they left us, they did an aileron rolls as their flaps came up and went into burners, and they quickly disappeared. Approach control at Cam Rahn Bay AFB instructed us to land and report to the Base Operations Officer. We did, and he really read me the riot act! He informed me that he could make me pay for the fuel the F-4s used, all because I did not know the secret daily password. I apologized profusely and finally got out of there, tongue-in-cheek. We all knew that I

Beech 18, N51259, of Air America awaits its customers at Danang AFB, South Vietnam, in March of 1968. (Robert Mikesh)

was a civilian, he was military, and he could do nothing about it, especially after he found out that I was Air America. He knew that all I had to do was to make a phone call and everything could be taken care of. I looked up the F-4 pilots later, and we had a good laugh over it all. Another successful mission!

Larry LaVerne
Air Force/Air America pilot

Beech 18, N51259, of Air America displays the standard color scheme of white over Navy blue. The white top lowered the interior temperature of the Beech 18 in the hot tropics of Southeast Asia. (Robert Mikesh)

Beech 18, N9073Z, of Air America visits Danang AFB in April of 1968. In the background is an Air America PC-6 Porter. (Robert Mikesh)

Beech Volpar turbo, N9956Z, was visiting Danang AFB, South Vietnam, in March of 1968. The Volpar was powered by two Garrett Air Research TPE-331-1-101B engines. Occasionally, Beech 18s nosed over on landings. They were sent to Tainen, and converted to Volpars by Air Asia, Ltd. When this occurred, 14 were built or converted there for Air America. One was lost in Laos. (Robert Mikesh)

The twin turbine engines of the Beech Volpar made the aircraft very fast, with a 202 knot cruising speed. Some pilots did not like that for their type of operations into some airfields that the customers needed to go. It got there too fast, and the pilots flew more missions as a result. It held 10 passengers. (Robert Mikesh)

The last three digits of all serial number registrations were repeated on the noses of all Air America aircraft with a few exceptions. 56Z on this nose means that the full registration was N9956Z. (Robert Mikesh)

Beech Volpar, N9671C, prepares for flight from Luang Pra Bang, Laos, in 1968. It carried 362 gallons of jet fuel, giving it an 8 hour endurance, or 1,336 nautical miles of range. On January 15, 1972, 71C was hit by an 85 mm anti-aircraft shell. Pilot Jim Rhyne lost his leg in that incident.

First Flight

One of the most vivid flights I remember was the very first one that I was on with Air America, and it went something like this.

I arrived in Vientiane, Laos, the day after my birthday in July of 1962. The monsoon rains were in full swing and no one met me as I deplaned. Air America people were there to meet someone else, told me they did not know I was coming, and I should go to town, find a place to live, and report to the field the next day. I did not know how to get to town or where to begin looking for a place to live.

Someone told me to go to the Constellation Hotel and see Maurice. I caught a Samlor to town and found Maurice. Maurice found a room for me at the Lido Hotel, which had occasional running water and less electricity. When the water did run, it had to run for a few minutes until the globs of mud ceased to chug out of the tap and you had a fairly constant spray of muddy water. It never cleared up better than muddy!

I went out to WatTai airport and I found I was to go on a flight with Joe Hazen in a Dornier Do-28. I had been hired to fly the Helio Courier, a single-engined STOL aircraft that I had never seen before. I got to see one for the first time the

day I went out to WatTai. A tough-looking bird, and I found out later it performed just as advertised.

I met Joe Hazen, we climbed into the Do-28 through the bat-wing doors for the cockpit seats, and he cranked up the engines and taxied out. There was no ATC clearance, just tower permission to take-off (if they were on the air), and a turn out to the North. We immediately were consumed by

Beech turbo Volpars were called Volpars by their crews. Here Volpar N9671C awaits its customers from a base in Thailand. Its maximum weight was 10,300 pounds.

overcast, climbing to about 7,000 feet. Joe leveled off and set up cruise conditions. We made turns to a new heading along the way to Sam Thong (LS 20) without any navigational aids. Just plain dead reckoning (heading, time, distance, and luck) for most of an hour. Then he eased the power back and began a blind descent. We broke out of the clouds in a small valley that had a red muddy landing site that Joe said was Sam Thong. It was about 1,000 feet long and had a pronounced rise about halfway down.

Joe put the Dornier down in the mud and stopped very quickly. We turned around and parked off the strip to get instructions for the day. Our first trip was to make an air drop to a new Helio strip where the Dornier could not land. We loaded the boxes and I was to be the kicker. I stayed in the back with the boxes and Joe got under way. We flew West for what seemed to be a long time in the soup, still with no navigational aids, and again Joe eased off and began a descent through the clouds. We saw the ground, and Joe must have seen something he recognized, because he took up a heading toward some mountains. On the side of one of these mountains was a Landing Site (LS), and they put out a ground signal. Joe told me when to drop the boxes, and I did as I was told. I had looked in the boxes, and they were toothbrushes! There was no toothpaste. I asked Joe what they were going to do with these and he said that he really did not know. It was part of the USAID program.

We really had not been flying in the clouds very long before I figured for sure that I could never learn my way around like these guys. I felt that they must have been born there to be able to find their way around as they were doing.

Volpar N9684C taxies back into the Air America ramp at Udorn, Thailand, in 1968 past a de Havilland Twin Otter, a Fairchild C-123, and a deHavilland DHC-4A Caribou .

Navigation training was the toughest part of the flying. If you miscalculated, you might hit a mountain or the enemy might shoot you down—neither was a good deal! The terrain was not easy—basically jungle, with mountains all over the country thrown in for good measure. The airport at Vientiane was 500 feet above sea level. Just 40 or so miles north was Ritaville Ridge at 5,500 feet above sea level. The terrain basically was up and down throughout the rest of the country. The mountains were 7,000 feet on up to 9,248 feet (PhuBia). I flew during check out and after check out in the monsoon clouds until September using dead reckoning below the moun-

Volpar turbo Beech, N6154U, awaits its customers at Danang AFB, South Vietnam, in August of 1966. Note the wide panoramic and large windows. (Tom Hansen)

This Beech 18 was in a beautiful Air America color scheme in the early 1960s. It was a scheduled passenger carrier.

tain tops, following courses through the mountains to a spot that I felt was correct for a let down to or near my destination. I must have been doing okay since I survived. The stark reality of what I was doing was suddenly driven home when the clouds disappeared in September at the end of the monsoon season. Now, I could see the mountains that I had been flying between, around, and over. It really got my attention.

The Helio Courier program was a very interesting one. The rest of the Air America pilots thought we were crazy, and so stated frequently. John Wiren, who arrived to work for Air America when I did, was in a Helio that suffered an engine failure in the early morning, and he crashed on a mountainside North of the Plain De Jars (PDJ).

He was unhurt, but he could not get a radio message off and operations did not miss him as they should have for be-

ing overdue. A Curtis C-46 flew right over him; the co-pilot was a new employee, and was learning the countryside. He saw the Helio and asked the pilot where this site was. The pilot banked the C-46, looked at the Helio, and told his co-pilot, "Those Helio pilots are nuts. They land before they even build the airstrips!" They continued on. At the end of the day as they were filling out their logs in Operations, everyone was asking if anyone had heard from John. The C-46 pilot questioned the co-pilot "Didn't we see a Helio somewhere today?"

The next morning, they sent a plane to the spot the C-46 crew had seen the Helio, and there sat John, more than a little pissed off that he had spent the night! It seems some natives came up to him after the crash wanting a ride to Vientiane. They must have thought it normal to land on the hillside and roll the airplane up into a ball!

I spent over twelve years flying with Air America, and it was an extremely interesting part of my life. I made many good friends and lost too many. It was an excellent group of people, a fine flying job, and we did a super job for the U.S. effort in that part of the world.

Jim Rhyne
Air America pilot.

A Sikorski UH-34 on a rice buying mission in northern Laos in 1968 attracts a large crowd of local Laotians. Numerous locations in Laos were accessible only by air drops or rotary-wing aircraft. The UH-34 was powered by a Wright R-1830-84C engine.

Sikorski S-58T, XW-PHD, retrieving parts from the crash site of an Air America Fairchild C-123K, 55-4555, that flew into a hill in very bad weather. Captain William Earl Reeves, J. M. Godahl, and 10 other customers were all killed in the crash. None of the Air America S-58Ts were in Vietnam—they all operated in Laos and Thailand only.

Some Typical Missions

During 1967, I was an Air force pilot who was "loaned" to Air America to fly C-7 Caribou missions. The missions consisted of "trash hauling" to include air drops of rice, pigs, cattle, ammunition, refugee relief, movement of indigenous personnel, and VIPs, to you name it. The Caribou was a well built airplane that was perfectly suited for the rigors of "off the beaten path" flying. The airplane has never gotten the praise that it deserves. We regularly operated in places no other aircraft (except maybe the Porter, but it did not carry that much) could. Our landing fields consisted of dirt roads, rice paddy dikes, dirt fields, PSP, and concrete. We were restricted from landing on water and in trees, although some tried it. The navigational aids were few to non-existent in Laos.

The landing gear was stressed to a 1,400 feet-per-minute rate of descent touchdown. Very few (if any) airplanes are capable of this, which made it an excellent STOL airplane. It can operate in places that an O-1 could not. We would land in the over-run at Tan Son Nhut AFB, near Saigon, Vietnam, and turn off the first taxiway. Or we could come over the end of a 10,000 foot runway at 1,000 feet and still land. This steep approach was useful in avoiding small arms fire to a 600 feet strip at a remote location.

A typical mission (if there was such a thing) was rice hauling. One fine day I was assigned to take four pallets of rice from Saigon to a Michelin rubber plantation north of Saigon.

After landing at a nearby dirt strip, I was met by a very polite but business-like Special Forces team. The NCO in charge asked what I was doing. I did not feel like it was any of his business, but I told him anyway. He said I cannot let you off-load that rice. He explained how the plantation workers were rubber workers by day and VC by night, and they had killed two of his men the previous night, and he sure as hell was not going to let the U.S. feed the bastards. Since the French

Laotian ground crew check the oil level on this UH-34 prior to another flight. Air America had one of the largest UH-34 fleets in the world at one time—topped only by some military air arms.

Sikorski S-58T, XW-P??, at Vientene, Laos, with Captain Stan Thompson in 1968, prepares for another mission. The S-58T was powered by a twin Pratt & Whitney PT6-T-3 engine combination, and cruised at 100 knots.

rubber plantations were off limits to U.S. people, he could not fire into them or give chase into them for fear of "upsetting our diplomatic relations with France." (It did not matter that the French supported North Vietnam as evidenced by the French ships in Haiphong harbor.) I explained to the Sergeant that I just had a mission to do and that I could not get involved in the policies of the situation (however, I did agree with him). I then told the loadmaster to offfload the rice. The sergeant pulled his .45 pistol, placed it to my head, and said he would kill me first. I told the loadmaster *not* to unload the rice! What a mess! I got on the radio to the office at Tan Son Nhut and advised them of the situation. The sergeant and I were ordered to offload the cargo and were told not to meddle in foreign policy. Since the sergeant was of the persuasive type (especially with the pistol pointed at my head), I rightfully agreed to leave with my rice. I took it back to Tan Son Nhut and unloaded it on the ramp. As it was late in the day, not many people were around and did not care anyway. I did not care either. I parked the Caribou and went to my billet. I never heard any more about it.

On another sunny day in Vietnam, I was enroute from a Montagnard area in the Central Highlands (where we had just air-dropped some pigs) to Pleiku. A desperate English speaking voice came up on the frequency 121.5VHF guard on the radio, "Cari-

bou over Kontum, Caribou over Kontum, do you read me?" I immediately answered, as I wanted to help if I could. A thankful voice from an Army unit replied "We have four 'ladies of the evening' that were flown in from Pleiku to spend a few days with us, and we were just advised by a friend at Headquarters that General X is enroute to our location in a Huey for a no-notice inspection. We have to get these ladies out of here right now! Can you land and take them to Pleiku? Please!" I told him that I was low on fuel and did not see how I could do it. He begged! He pleaded! I landed! We made an engine-running onload of the four Vietnamese lovelies. They were smiling and happy, but confused as to why they were leaving early. As we were taxiing out, the General was landing. I took the ladies to Pleiku. I am sure the guys at Kontum were eternally grateful. I hope they passed inspection. Another successful mission!

Initially I was concerned about the inhumane method of air-dropping live animals. The Vet explained to me that some of the animals had a heart attack and died as soon as they hit the slipstream, so they were dead when they hit the ground. They were going to be butchered anyway, so...

Two of us were air-dropping somewhere when the lead Caribou started receiving ground fire. He yelled over the radio to get out of there, but I was already configured for the drop, so I decided to go ahead and drop. We returned to base as we were inspecting for small arms damage. The other pilot showed me his Zippo lighter, which had been lying on the center console. A bullet had penetrated the lighter, and the lighter still worked. The radio did not, though. The center console was between the pilot and the co-pilot, a distance of about 15 inches. I thought the lighter still working was neat, so we took a picture of it working and sent it along with an explanation to Zippo, thinking it would be a good advertisement! However, we never heard from them. I guess the anti-war sentiment at the time did not help. Another successful mission.

Larry LaVerne
Air Force/Air America pilot

Most Sikorski UH-34s and S-58Ts were standard colors of the U.S. Marines of flat overall olive drab. The aft transmission housing was usually yellow. If the Sikorski was civilian registered, it was on the nose in black. Other markings were on the tail showing an H (meaning helicopter) followed by two numbers, ie H-12. (Ward Reimer)

Bell 204, N1304X, (a UH-1B), prepares for takeoff from a landing pad at Saigon, South Vietnam, on February 25, 1970. Note that just after the title of Air America on the tail is a red kangaroo "zap," which means that the Bell probably visited Vung Tau, South Vietnam, where the majority of the Australians were stationed. They were "imfamous" for zapping all visiting aircraft. (Bob Livingstone)

A Bell 204 of Air America sling-loads an item in November of 1967 at Pleiku, South Vietnam. (Author)

Bell 205 (UH-ID), XW-PD?, prepares to sling-load a Wright R-1830 engine pod from a Sikorski UH-34. Note the crew member hanging out the door, and a ground handler on the engine preparing to hook it on. The location is LS-16 in Laos.

Bell 204, XW-PFH, retrieves a man on a hoist from the jungle. Air America flew a wide variety of missions in support of American aims and goals in Southeast Asia.

Aircraft Maintenance with Air America

The aircraft maintenance organization and its policies with the companies of Air America, Civil Air Transport, Southern Air Transport, Bird and Sons, Continental Airlines Service, Inc., and Air Asia, was the result of a continual refinement program, through the efforts of many many people rather than one single individual.

The principles in the implementation of the maintenance organizations and their success over the years were Hugh Crundy (who later became the President of Air America), Al Weuste, George Stubbs (Director, Regional Maintenance Department), Doc Lewis, Jim Burkett, George Morrison, C.Y. Wei, and hundreds of others who shall remain nameless because of space limitations, but are not forgotten by the rest.

Maintenance and its personnel were interchangeable from one situation to another, or from one station to another, without long training requirements or familization with the new location—communications, quality control, the paperwork—the entire organizational structure was identical. The major change was, most often, the airline name on your shirt.

Aircraft maintenance was essentially split into two sections—the base maintenance at Tainen was headed up by John Berry, who was responsible for the entire company fleet, in teams of heavy service modifications, and major damage repairs and battle damage, along with its military and commercial overhaul business.

The Regional Maintenance Department (RMD) was headed by George Stubbs, who was responsible for all field operations at some 17 locations from Japan to all of Southeast Asia, with hundreds of personnel, which, at one time, included thirty-three different nationalities. The administrative assistant to George Stubbs was Thelma Liu, who was effectively called the "Dragon Lady" by the employees at Tainen. Milton Caniff, of "Terry and the Pirates" fame, used Thelma and the company for much of his material in his famous comic strip.

Base maintenance at Tainan and its massive support shops, engineering, supply, ground support, etc., were tied into regional maintenance through George Stubbs. Far field support teams or individuals were always available for backup. This "hand in glove" relationship between the two sections was the key to the operating success of the company, without which nothing would have moved.

The field personnel, or out-stations, were the end users. The managers, supervisors, crew chiefs, mechanics, and the hundreds of other support personnel, were the last part of the puzzle—the key to making it all work. The "ontime" and "numbers of aircraft available" to the customer on a daily basis speaks for itself at all locations.

The pilots, as we know, are legendary—the flight mechanics have, for the most part, become the unsung hags. Their performance up-country, often under the most adverse conditions, under enemy fire, without parts or support, except for a radio, still managed to bring back the aircraft using some very ingenious repairs. Some of these make-shift repairs were infamous!

The credit for the success of the maintenance effort over the many years must be given to George Stubbs, C.Y. Wei, and John Bary, who were tireless in their efforts and who set examples by their dedication to duty for the rest of us to follow throughout the remainder of our lives!

Ward Reimer
Air America maintenance

A Bell 204 of Air America delivers a customer to a heliport next to the Mekong River near Saigon in 1967.

Bell 204, N8511F, of Air America, parked on the Air America ramp at Danang AFB, South Vietnam, in March of 1968. Navy blue and white or silver made for a beautiful color scheme. (Robert Mikesh)

A Douglas C-47, B-817, visits Danang AFB, South Vietnam, in March of 1968. The Douglas C47/DC-3 series was with Air America and CAT from the very beginning along with the Curtis C-46. (Robert Mikesh)

Douglas C-47, B-559, lands at Danang AFB in late 1968. Numerous C-47s came and went during the life-span of Air America. Most were of Chinese registry. (William Booth)

A Douglas C-47, or DC-3, at Cam Ram Bay, South Vietnam, in 1971, in the markings of Continental Air Services, Inc. (CASI). CASI was a very close cousin to Air America, and flew similar types of missions. CASI was a much smaller operation than Air America. This color scheme is almost identical to Continental Airlines at that time. (Tom Hansen)

Air Cambodia Douglas C-47, N83AC (American registered), operating over the Mekong River that flows through Cambodia to South Vietnam. Air America provided maintenance for other customers that had no facilities or skilled workers.

Dornier DO-28, N2001F, visits Danang AFB, South Vietnam, in March of 1968. The DO-28 had great twin-engine STOL performance, which was needed for some of the short, high landing strips in northern Laos. (Robert Mikesh)

The Dornier DO-28 had a unique engine and landing gear arrangement that worked very well. The visibility from the Dornier DO-28 was fantastic. (Robert Mikesh)

The control surfaces on the DO-28 were very large for STOL operations at low speed. They were operated by Air America in small numbers for many years, but most were retired by 1968. (Robert Mikesh)

Dornier DO-28, N2001F, is ready for boarding by crew and customers. Note the large entrances for the crew and customers as shown here at Ban Me Thuot, South Vietnam, in March of 1964.

Dornier DO-28, B-931, was a Chinese registered aircraft that had a slightly different color scheme and no Air America titles, although it was operated by Air America. B-931 was on the Air America ramp at Danang AFB, South Vietnam, in November of 1966. (Tom Hansen)

Dornier DO-28, N4224C, suffered a hard landing with the left engine running. Very little damage was done at LS-13 (Ban Na, Laos). Note the passenger window modification (a very small viewing area). This aircraft was originally operated by Bird & Sons, before being transferred to CASI and then to Air America.

Air America pilot Dick Chambers, watching the loading of his Dornier DO-28 somewhere in Laos in 1968.

Dornier DO-28 with French registry, F-OBYR, at Quan Loi, South Vietnam, near the Cambodian border, in March of 1971. It is unknown why this aircraft had French registry when most Air America DO-28s were U.S. or Chinese registered. (Author)

De Havilland DHC-4 Caribou, N539Y, was based at Tan Son Nhut AFB, South Vietnam, which is very near Saigon. This February 1967 photograph was taken on the Air America ramp. (Author)

The STOL capabilities of the Caribou are legendary. The large rudder gave very good low speed control. N539Y was always bare metal its entire tenure with Air America. (Robert Mikesh)

Laotian soldiers and ground crew members of Air America push a Helio Courier out of the way as an Air America Caribou prepares to take off from the small airstrip in Laos.

The only known Chinese registered Caribous were B-853, B-171, B-393, and B-382. It is also unique in that it was painted overall gray and not bare metal. B-853 was leaving for a mission from Danang AFB, South Vietnam, in March of 1968 when photographed. (Robert Mikesh)

Caribou, N539Y, landing at a hard-surfaced runway, was probably in South Vietnam. Usually they operated out of rougher, shorter, uneven landing strips that were much more remote.

DHC Caribou, N581PA, belonged to Pacific Architects & Engineering (PA&E) as shown in Vung Tau, South Vietnam, in 1970. PA&E built bridges, industrial plants, etc., and had close ties to Air America. (Bob Livingstone)

Caribou, N544Y, at Tan Son Nhut AFB, South Vietnam, in January of 1970, along with N539Y, were based at Saigon during the war. Air America is barely visible under the fuselage windows by the lowered flaps. N544Y is still flying in Africa doing relief work. (Bob Livingstone)

DHC-4A, number B-382, is bare metal with black lettering and numbers at Vientene, Laos, parked next to two C-123Ks of the Royal Lao Air Force. The RLAF received 12 C-123Ks in 1973.

Caribou, N539Y, was the most photographed Air America Caribou, since it was operated out of Tan Son Nhut AFB, South Vietnam, for many years as illustrated here in June of 1968. American GIs carried cameras all around their tour of duty. (Robert Mikesh)

DHC Caribou, N539Y, survived Air America and the Vietnam war. It was being operated in Alaska in February of 1978 at Anchorage, Alaska, as shown here. Only the name Air America had been removed. All other markings are the same after it was sold by Air America in 1976. It later crashed and burned in Lime Village, Alaska, in 1986. (Author)

A Caribou "on loan" from the U.S. Air Force from Vietnam. It has the standard Southeast Asia color scheme, but no U.S. insignia. The Caribou is 60-3762, and was the first production Caribou delivered to the U.S. Army. Full-span flaps made for impressive STOL performance.

Caribou, B-171, ran off of the landing strip in Laos. It was probably over-loaded. It was repaired and flew again. The full-span flaps were huge.

The Porter was one of the most recognizable aircraft operated by Air America. Porter N355F is shown here at Vientene, Laos, in 1968. Note the CASI Curtis C-46 in the background.

Caribou, B-393, crashed at LS-14 when it tried to go around after a bad approach. LS-14 was not a "go around" strip due to the rugged surrounding terrain. The crew walked away, unscratched. The weather conditions changed dramatically very quickly in Laos. The Caribou was parted-out.

Pilatus Porter PC-6C, N195X, returning from a mission with a broken tailwheel, which was the Porter's weak point. Air America aircraft were shot at continually where ever they operated. There were some losses.

Porter N367F at Udorn, Thailand, was parked on the Air America ramp in front of the base manager's office. Since the tailwheel was the weak point on the Porter, some aircraft were modified with a deflector bar in front of the assembly as shown here. It was called the Air America cowcatcher.

Porter N359F crashed on landing after a very steep descent into a Laotian LS. It was repaired and flew again. The Porter was a very rugged aircraft.

Porter N358F tied down at a large air base in Southeast Asia. The Porters operated by Air America used four different engines. This is powered by a Garrett Air Research engine, and was the last and best of the four types of engines used. (Don Logan)

PC-6C Porter, N748N, on short final at an airbase in Southeast Asia, reveals empty seats in the passenger section. Another mission successfully completed. The motto of Air America was "Anything, Anywhere, Anytime, Professionally."

Porter PC-6B, N383R, taxies back to the Air America ramp at Tan Son Nhut AFB, South Vietnam, near Saigon in September of 1966. The B model had an early Turbomeca engine that was extremely loud. (Author)

Porter N12235 of Air America awaits its next customers in October of 1966 at Nha Trang AFB, South Vietnam. This Porter was powered by the Turbomeca Asazou engine. The Porter was equipped with oversized wheels, and it tolerated un-prepared and muddy airfields very well. (Author)

Porter N184L taxies out past an USAF Fairchild C-123 in September of 1966 at Tan Son Nhut AFB, near Saigon. The Porter had excellent visibility from the front seats for the flight crew. A Porter cruised at 120 knots. (Author)

PC-6B Porter N184L of Air America at Danang AFB, South Vietnam, in October of 1966, shows its early Turbomeca engine, which was the PC-6B. The PC-6A was powered by a Lycoming piston engine, and the PC-6C was powered by the Garrett Air Research TPE-331-25—the same engine as on the Beech Volpar conversion. There was also a Pratt & Whitney PT-6A powered Porter. (Tom Hansen)

Porter N198X awaits its next mission from a crude dirt landing strip. A Porter could carry 9 people.

Porter N393R returns from another successful mission in September of 1966 to the Air America ramp at Tan Son Nhut AFB, South Vietnam. An Air America C-47 is in the background. (Author)

Porter N291R begins another flight in September of 1966 from the Air America ramp at Tan Son Nhut AFB. Notice the four Air America Beech 18s in the background. The wide span of the landing gear on the Porter made for very stable landings. (Author)

Porter N393R at Can Tho AFB, South Vietnam, in 1971 shows the Garrett Air Research engine. It was significantly quieter than the older Turbomeca Astezou-powered Porters. The Porter could takeoff in 300 feet. It carried 128 gallons of jet fuel that lasted about three hours. (Tom Hansen)

Another Pilatus Porter with its very loud Turbomeca Astazou engine awaits the next mission at Tan Son Nhut AFB, South Vietnam, in February of 1967. The wide cabin doors allowed ease of entry and exit for people or cargo. (Author)

Porter N393R takes off from the Hue Citadel airport in January of 1968, days before the battle for the city and the Tet offensive began. (Robert Kikesh)

Porter N391R rests on the Air America ramp at Danang AFB, South Vietnam, in March of 1968, next to an Air America Beech 18. (Robert Mikesh)

Pilatus Porter PC-6 N393R departs for another mission in January of 1968 from the Hue Citadel airport. The Porter was a very rugged aircraft designed and built in Switzerland. (Robert Mikesh)

Porter, XW-PDI, was one of the few Laotian registered Porters. It was also shown on the Air America rosters of aircraft, showing the "fluidity" of aircraft between some companies like Air America, the USAF, and Continental Air Services, Inc. (CASI), of which this Porter belonged at the time of the photograph. XW-PDI was powered by a Pratt & Whitey PT6A-27 engine.

For extremely small and short landing strips, Air America operated numerous Helio Couriers. B857 was a Chinese registered Helio Courier, shown here visiting Danang AFB, South Vietnam, in March of 1968. (Robert Mikesh)

Just taxiing out from the Air America ramp at Tan Son Nhut AFB, near Saigon, in September of 1967, B-857 has just passed the C-123 Provider flight line next to the Air America ramp. (Author)

Helio model H-395 Super Courier, number B-857, visits Danang AFB in March of 1968. The black triangle under the wing is an anti-reflection marking for the landing light. (Robert Mikesh)

Helio B-857 was Chinese registered. The full-span leading-edge slats helped give the Courier tremendous STOL performance. The location is Tan Son Nhut AFB, South Vietnam, in September of 1967. (Author)

Courier B-869 awaits its customers at Phu Loi, South Vietnam, in February of 1967. In the background are numerous fuel bladders for air lifting fuel to remote areas, usually by CH-47 Chinook helicopters. (Author)

After a very short take off run, an Air America Courier becomes airborne. The flaps were almost full span. Coupled with the full-span leading-edge slats, tremendous lift is generated, getting the Courier airborne very rapidly.

Courier XW-PCD was Laotian registered. It also had a Laotian insignia on the wings and tail in red and white colors. A high angle of attack landing bent the tail. This happened at LS-20 in Laos. LS-20 was Sam Thong, Laos.

Helio Courier B-857 on the Air America ramp at Danang AFB, South Vietnam, in March of 1968, shows its very large control surfaces for STOL operations. In the background is an Air America Beech 18. (Robert Mikesh)

Courier 861, which is really B-861, flies along over the Plain Of Jars in Laos. The landing gear is not wide in flight or touch-down, but it spreads when the lift dies.

Ed Staricha, pilot, awaits his customers at an LS in Laos. The Courier is XW-PGB, one of several Laotian registered Couriers. Most Air America crew wore gray or white shirts and epaulets with stripes.

All Helio Super Couriers were bare metal with black markings and anti-glare panels. This Chinese registered Courier does not have the B before the registration number, which indicates an early (pre1962) photograph.

Although there is no Air America name on this Courier (this was a fairly common occurrence), it was flown and operated by Air America. Courier B-857 is taxiing by the U.S. Army's 1st Signal Brigade aviation support area at Tan Son Nhut AFB, South Vietnam, in September of 1967. (Author)

Helio Courier B-869 at Phu Loi, South Vietnam, in February of 1967, is next to barrels in the background that are POL (petroleum, oil, lubricant) containers. (Author)

An Air America Helio Courier loads up some Laotian customers at a mountain top airstrip in northern Laos.

Helio Courier 845 (later B-845) of Air America atop a mountain airstrip in Laos with some passengers standing by with some cargo, stops at the end of the runway. The fog in the valleys was some of the fast changing weather conditions that had to be dealt with for operation in Laos.

Some Helio Couriers, including 857 and 863 (later B-857 and B-863), were at Maung Ouh, Laos, during an effort to find another Helio that was shot down.

Preparing for a search and rescue mission at LS-50 in Laos are a variety of helicopters. Shown are two Bell 205s (UH-IDs), and two Sikorski UH-34s.

Fairchild C-123K, 55-4556, of Air America, undergoes a 100-hour phase inspection maintenance at Udorn, Thailand. Only the numbers 556 are displayed on the nose and tail in black. (Ward Reimer)

Fairchild C-123K, 55-4555, at LS-11 on September 20, 1971, skidded off the runway after blowing a tire. The pilots were Captain James F. Vogles, and flight officer Ernst L. Terry. It was repaired and flew again.

The nose gear collapsed on Fairchild C-123K, 55-4524, in February of 1971 at LS-190. It was easily repaired and flown out. Air America C-123s were bare metal with only the flag on the tail, and a very small Air America on the fuselage under the wings.

Fairchild C-123K, 55-4545, at Phan Rang AFB, South Vietnam, in June of 1970, is bare metal with a very small Air America just barely visible under the wing's jet pod on the fuselage. (Bob Livingstone)

The last three numbers of the U.S. Air Force serial numbers were used on all C-123s operated by Air America. 374 is actually C-123B-18-FA, 56-4374, when it visited Danang AFB, South Vietnam, in May of 1967. (Tom Hansen)

Air America operated a few Boeing-Vertol CH-47 Chinook helicopters is standard U.S. Army color schemes. Only the last three digits of the serial number were used for identification. 857 was actually CH-47C 68-15857 as shown here at Udorn, Thailand. Chinooks were powered by two Lycoming T55-11A engines.

Local Thai personnel conduct engine maintenance on this Air America CH-47C at Udorn, Thailand. 998 was actually CH-47C, 68-15998. Chinooks operated by Air America were not used in Vietnam, but only in Laos. (Ward Reimer)

XW-PGR was a Boeing 307—the first pressurized airliner, and a passenger version of the B-17—is shown here in Royal Air Lao markings. Note that the outboard portion of the wing is missing. PGR was a frequent visitor to Air America facilities and was a very common sight at various LS or landing sights around Laos. One Boeing 307 was shot down.

The Royal Air Lao Boeing 307 (one of only 10 built—all before 1941) was hit by a taxiing military Douglas C-47 of the Royal Lao Air Force at LS-54 on April 20, 1971. Since spare parts for the Boeing 307 were non-existent, the 307 was cut up into many large pieces for scrap. The Boeing 307s were owned and operated by Asalier Zur, a French company out of Paris, and headed up by Gene Albray. They had three Boeing 307s, and were leased to the UN Polish inspection team, who made weekly trips to Hanoi.

The Hughes OH-6A Cayuse of Air America was in standard U.S. Army color scheme, as shown here on the Air America ramp at Pakse, Laos, in 1973. Air America obtained two OH-6As in April of 1972.

Piper Super Cub, XW-PEM, was based at Udorn, Thailand, and flown by Air America in the standard Piper color scheme. Jerry McPherson was the pilot. It was white with red markings. It was used to train Hmong personnel to fly. They were selected and then taught English, and taught to fly by Jerry in this Super Cub. Then they progressed on to the North American T-28. They did a great job for the Laotian Air Force. Jerry bought the Super Cub later, when it was no longer needed.

DeHavilland DHC-6 Twin Otter N774M was the first production DHC-6-300. Air America had four and CASI had five. Most were delivered in 1971. Air America lost two. The landing gear broke off on landing at LS-32, having hit the lip of the runway. N774M was equipped with an AP-115 terrain following radar, as was another DHC-6-300, N5662, which later crashed on July 23, 1972.

Air America operated for a short time three modified On Mark conversions of the B-26 Invader, called "The Executive." It was air conditioned, pressurized, and had a Douglas DC-6 or DC-7 windshield, and fuselage as evident by the windows. It had Pratt & Whitney R-2800 CH-16/17 engines off of a DC-6. This aircraft was modified to have a rear cargo drop door, and it had AP-99 terrain following radar installed. Six pilots were checked out to fly them, including Frank Bonansinga and Jim Rhyne. (Frank Bonansigna)

Vientene, Laos, was supposedly a neutral city in a neutral country. Of course, it was anything but that. Therefore, it was common to see Russian aircraft parked next to American aircraft. This is an Aeroflot IL-18 visiting Vientene on August 20, 1971.

A de Havilland Rapide, XW-TA?, was at Van Vieng, Laos. This was probably operated by Air America, but was a bizarre aircraft for Laos (it was registered in Laos), since it was built out of wood and canvas, and would not have lasted very long in the tropical moisture of Southeast Asia. It was in the late 1960s that this DH-98A nosed over upon landing.

Another aircraft of a bizarre nature in Laos was a Scottish Aviation Twin Pioneer that skidded off the end of the runway at LS-48. It had two R-1340 engines. Air America did not operate the Twin Pioneer, but Continental Air Services, Inc. (CASI) had three of them. The second one went into the Mekong River, and the third became a restaurant in Vientene, Laos!

Two USAF Sikorski CH-53s, probably of the 21st Special Operation Squadron (SOS) at an airfield at Muong Soui, Laos, in Spetember of 1971 during Operation Golden Mountain. Air America did not operate any of the CH-53s, but flew in support of the operations.

Dornier DO-28B-1, N9180X, (serial number 3181 that was built in 1964), in non-standard Air America markings, visits Ban Som Thuong, Xieng Khoung Province, Laos, on January 9, 1966. It was part of the massive 30-plus aircraft used to carry guests to the Hmong/Meo New Year's celebrations.

Dornier DO-28A-1, XW-PCG, of Air America, landing at Thakhek, Laos, in 1966. It was originally registered at N4228G. It was damaged, repaired, and re-registered as XW-PDB on January 22, 1966, or earlier.

Dornier DO-28A-1, XW-PCG, of Air America, parked at Thakhek in central Laos on November 15, 1965. A Vietnamese dragon is drawn on the fuselage. XW-PCG is serial number 3026, and was built in Fredrickshafen, Germany, in 1961. It was registered as N4222G earlier in 1965.

Douglas C-47D, number 999, at Thakhek in central Laos in 1966, is taxiing out for another mission. The nose and tail number 999 were the only markings. 999 was actually 45-0999.

Douglas C-47B, number 147, was actually 43-16147 of Air America, although the only visible markings are the numbers. The nose numbers were added in June of 1966. 147 is shown landing at Thakhek in central Laos in 1966.

Douglas C-47B, number 147, is being loaded up for another scheduled passenger and freight mission out of Thakhek in 1966.

Douglas C-47D, number 994, was actually 45-0994. The name Air America was added in June of 1966, and the serial number was added at that time on the nose. The Volkswagen was operated by the Laotians, the white Land Cruiser was operated by the British, and the green Jeep Wagoneer was operated by the American USAID agency.

Pilatus PC-6B Porter, XW-PCL, was powered by a Pratt & Whitney PT-6A engine. It is just rolling on take-off from Sam Thuong airfield in Xieng Khouang Province in Laos on January 6, 1966. This was part of the Air America massive airlift of over 30 aircraft to take customers from Vientene to the Hmong/Meo New Year's cerebration.

DHC-4A Caribou 392 (actually 61-2392) and 389 (actually 61-2389) of Air America at Ban Son Thuong in central Laos on January 9, 1966, awaits their return passengers from the celebration on the new Hmong/Meo New Year.

Curtis C-46F-1-CU, N4871V, was built as 44-78587, and delivered to the USAAF on July 11, 1945. It went to Chungking, China, where CAT bought it. By 1964, it had been transferred to Bird and Sons, Inc. Later it went to Continental Air Service, Inc. (CASI). It is shown derelict here at Vientene, Laos in 1965. Note that the Laotian Air Force insignia was carried on it.

Helio Courier, XW-PEA, is just landing at Thakhek in central Laos in 1966. 541 was barely visible on the fin, even though it was removed.

Fairchild C-123B Provider, N5007X, of Air America is unloading supplies at Luang Prabang, Laos, in early 1966. This C-123 was being used as a passenger and freight aircraft.

Bird and Sons, Inc., later Continental Air Services, Inc. (CASI), operated three Scottish Aviation Twin Pioneer STOL aircraft. CASI later took them out of service. XW-PBP was visiting Ban Sam Thuong in central Laos on January 9, 1966. The light blue oval contained the letters PAL—Philippines Air Lines, but was over-painted. XW-PBP was a passenger aircraft. A second "Twin Pin" was XW-PBJ, and was a rice-dropper in identical markings. The Continental Airlines logo is barely visible above the blue strip next to the oval.

Air America UH-34D, H-12, on the football (soccer) field at Luang Probang, Laos, in 1966. It was to this soccer field that the French wounded soldiers were evacuated by French Sikorski H-19s from Dien Bien Phu in 1954.

Porter XW-PCL of CASI is taking off from Ban Som Thuong, Xieng Khuang Province, in central Laos on January 9, 1966. Other aircraft visible include Twin Pioneer XW-PBD, Caribous 389 and 392, a single Twin Pioneer XL665, a British embassy aircraft on loan from No. 209 Squadron based at Singapore, a Helio Courier, two olive drab UH-34s of Air America, two white UH-34s of the International Control Commission (ICC), and a Beech 18.

The Air America ramp at Vientene, Laos, on August 11, 1966, shows a Curtis C-46 Commando, a Douglas C-47D number 994 (actually 45-0994), Caribou number 392 (actually 61-2392), and a wrecked Porter, N9444.

Boeing 727-092C, N5093, serial number 19175, was bought by CAT, and delivered on December 10, 1966. It is shown here at Tan Son Nhut AFB, near Saigon, in February of 1967, displaying Southern Air Transport markings, illustrating the "fluidity" of aircraft between companies owned by the Pacific Corporation. On January 3, 1968, it was re-registered as B-1018 with CAT—Civil Air Transport. On February 16, 1968, it crashed 7 miles northwest of Taipei while on approach with 21 fatalities. In its 14 months of service, the 727 flew 3,918 hours. 42 passengers survived the crash. This crash was the demise of CAT. (Author)

A Southern Air Transport Douglas DC-6 unloads its cargo at Tan Son Nhut AFB, South Vietnam, near Saigon in October of 1966. (Author)

This was not a C-130, but a Lockheed L-100, model 382B-14C, registered as N9266R, serial number 4250. It was the last of six L-100s delivered to National Leasing in December of 1968. It was operated by Southern Air Transport, as well as Saturn Airways, Alaska International, and Air Algeria. It was blown up by a mine while taking off from Wau, Sudan, on September 2, 1991, with the International Red Cross. Over the years, Southern Air Transport operated 22 Lockheed L-100/C-130 type of aircraft. CASI operated two L-100s, but only for the first six months of 1966 before disposing of them. All Air America L-100/C-130s, with one exception, were "on loan" C-130s from the USAF. (Author)

XW-TAC was a Douglas DC-4 or C-54 operated out of Vientene, Laos, by Royal Air Lao. Although Air America had no connections with the airline, they operated side-by-side in the area, and probably assisted them with the maintenance of the aircraft. The Laotian flag on the tail is red and white elephants.

XW-TAF was a Douglas C-47 or DC-3 that also operated out of Vientene, Laos. Again Air America had no connection with the airline, but probably provided some maintenance support. They were not in competition with each other.

The two Porters parked on a ramp awaiting their customers are N12450 and N135K.

De Havilland of Canada DHC-4A Caribou, N539Y, was based at Tan Son Nhut AFB, South Vietnam, for years. It survived the war only to later crash in Alaska in 1986.

DHC-6-300 Twin Otter of Air America is towed past a UH-34D 9364 (actually BuNo 149364) of the Royal Cambodian Air Force at Udorn AFB, Thailand, in 1973. This Twin Otter had the "night flying color scheme" with radar nose, which is just a little rounder than a normal Twin Otter.

Sikorksi UH-34Ds of Air America are undergoing outdoor maintenance at Udorn AFB, Thailand, in 1973. (Ward Reimer)

Air America had one of the largest fleets of Sikorski H-34s in the world in the early 1970s. The UH34 in the foreground is from the Royal Cambodian Air Force. The other two H-34s belong to Air America. The center H-34 has long range fuel tanks mounted on it. This is the Air America ramp at Udorn AFB, Thailand about 1970. (Ward Reimer)

Sikorski S-58T, XW-PHB, of Air America rests on the ramp at Udorn AFB, Thailand, awaiting its next mission in 1970. (Ward Reimer)

The Air America ramp at Udorn AFB, Thailand, in 1970 was a very busy location. In the foreground is a UH-34, number H-67, of Air America, being towed toward an Air America S-58T and Bell 205, XW- PFH. (Ward Reimer)

The Beech 18 was the civilian version of the C-45. N9592Z was involved in a minor mishap in the late 1960s. It was easily repaired and placed back into service. No one was hurt. They were not easy to ground loop. (Ward Reimer)

Piper Apache, N3277P, suffered a nose-gear failure in Saigon in 1963. It was easily repaired. N3277P was originally owned by Dr. Thomas Dooley, who was the hill tribe doctor who treated the Hmongs, Meos, and others. He was quite famous, and wrote many books about his experiences. (Ward Reimer)

Piper N3183P is actually a Geronimo conversion of the Apache. It was originally owned by Max Conrad of Minnesota, who flew it around the world in the late 1950s. Air America later sold it to a man in Stockholm, Sweden. (Ward Reimer)

Presently, Piper N3183P is still being operated and is based in California. 83P had a large dorsel fin and a long nose. In the photograph, it is being refueled at Udorn AFB, Thailand, in the mid-1960s. (Ward Reimer)

Aero Commander 560, Serial number 2714, was at Udorn AFB, Thailand, for maintenance. This aircraft was given to the King of Laos by America as a present for continued support. In the background is a CASI Curtis C-46.

Aero Commander 560, serial number 2714, was, at one time, the personal aircraft of President Eisenhower. Ike used it for flying from Washington to his farm near Gettysburg, Pennsylvania. The King of Laos really liked his gift from the USA. Air America provided the maintenance for it.

Caribou 393 at Udorn AFB, Thailand, sits on the PSP ramp to begin service again to the customers. In the left background are parts of an McDonnell F-4 Phantom jet fighter showing the tail marking OZ. OZ was the tail code for the 14th Tactical Reconnaissance Squadron of the 432nd Tactical Reconnaissance Wing. The fin cap was red.

Fairchild C-123K, number 617, was actually 54-0617. It was undergoing maintenance at the Air America facilities at Udorn AFB, Thailand. Air America provided support for most of the Royal Lao Air Force aircraft. The insignia was red and white.

Fairchild C-123K, number 386, taxies out for another mission for the Royal Lao Air Force. 386 is actually 56-4386.

Royal Laotian Air Force North American T-28A, serial number 51-7635, is being pre-flighted by its crew. On the pylons are two 250 pound bombs, two 500 pound bombs, and two .50 cal. machine gun pods. Air America pilots trained some of the Laotian pilots to fly the T-28. Some became very famous, like Hmong pilot Ly Lue, whose skill and daring were infamous.

North American T-28, BuNo 140533, at LS-20 (LS-20 was Sam Thong, Laos), is parked near a Porter PC-6C of Air America. The T-28 is operated in close conjunction with Air America rescue operations.

A med-evac helicopter landed on top of Dornier DO-28, N2002F, while the Air America Dornier was taking off. Everyone made it out with few injuries. The Dornier was built strong, but not that strong. The cabin is still intact after the accident. (Ward Reimer)

Sikorski UH-34, numbered H-70, with Air America, was shot down over Laos. Very little of it remains except for the aft tail with the tail rotor (in the center), and the engine on the far right. It was a dangerous area to operate aircraft over Laos. Air America had 243 fatalities during their operations from 1959 until 1975. (Ward Reimer)

Beech 18, 92Z, nosed over upon landing at Tan Son Nhut AFB, South Vietnam, near Saigon. Minor damage occurred, and it was back in the air in a short amount of time. (Ward Reimer)

Beech 18, N9673Z, landed in a marsh. It was lifted out by an Air America CH-47 from Udorn AFB, Thailand, and easily repaired. (Ward Reimer)

Beech 18, N5254V, rolled over and landed inverted on August 16, 1965. No one was injured, and all got out without injury. (Ward Reimer)

Curtis C-46, B-156, was written off upon landing where the wing was torn off. There was a small fire inside of the fuselage, but everybody got out without injury. (Ward Reimer)

When Curtis C-46, B-156, crash-landed, the engines were not operating. The C-46 was a very strongly built aircraft, and it remained virtually intact when it crashed. (Ward Reimer)

Curtis C-46F, B-156, was one of the original C-46s bought for CAT operations in the 1940s. Its entire flying career was spent in the Orient flying first for the USAAF, then CAT, and finally Air America. (Ward Reimer)

Curtis C-46D-20-CU was originally built as 44-78413. When originally operated by CAT, it was registered as XT-810 in the late 1940s. Later it was registered as B-860, and even later as B-912 with Air America. This color scheme was white and navy blue. The photograph was taken in the mid 1950s at a U.S. Air Force base.

Convair 880-22M-4 was delivered to CAT on June 16, 1961, and registered as B-1008. It was later traded to Boeing for a 727-092C. It was later owned by Cathay Pacific Airways, and based in Hong Kong in January of 1968. It was promoted with CAT as the Mandarin jet. This is the color scheme in 1965 on the Convair. It was scrapped at Seletar in June of 1984.

Douglas C-54A-DO, B-1002, was originally built for the USAAF as 41-37287 in May of 1943. It was one of the first C-54s built. It was then transferred to the U.S. Navy as BuNo 39141 and operated in the Pacific area. After the war, it was operated by Philippines Air Lines as PI-C108. CAT obtained it in 1947 and re-registered it as NC86552, and changed it in 1953 to B-1002, a Chinese registration. This color scheme shows a beautiful dragon on the fuselage.

Douglas DC-6B, B-1006, was delivered to CAT on September 30, 1958. It was almost the last DC-6 built (line number was 1032, serial number was 45550). This 1961 photograph is in Hong Kong, where it operated regularly. The international passenger service was known as the "Mandarin Flight."

When B-1006 was delivered to CAT, it had this beautiful oriental dragon on the nose. CAT transferred the DC-6B to Royal Air Lao in 1968, and it was re-registered as XW-PFZ. It was later transferred to Southern Air Transport where it was converted into a cargo hauler in September of 1973. At that time, it was registered as N93459. In 1978, it was sold to Trans Continental Airlines. It is still flying as G-SIXC with Air Atlantique based in Coventry, England.

Pacific Architects and Engineering (PA&E) was a large construction company that built airfields, roads, factories, etc., throughout Southeast Asia. In order to support its far-flung operations, they had some aircraft, including Caribou N581PA. PA&E was owned by the Pacific Corporation, who also owned Air America.

Caribou 401 of Air America taxies in from another mission to a large air base in Southeast Asia. 401 is unusual in that it has weather radar installed in the nose.

Caribou N539Y, along with Caribou N544Y, were purchased factory-fresh from de Havilland of Canada by Air America. Ward Reimer was the Air America representative. Both Caribous were stationed at Tan Son Nhut AFB near Saigon, South Vietnam. Both survived the war, and N544Y is still hauling cargo in Africa.

An Air America Beech 18 was involved in a landing accident with a parked U.S. Army Grumman OV-1 Mohawk in South Vietnam in the late 1960s. The Grumman was a write-off. The Beech appears to be salvageable. (Patrick Martin)

Porter N285L taxies out of a rough gravel ramp in Laos carrying Naval Intelligence officers on a classified mission.

Convair 880M was to give CAT an update and modernization, but it was traded in on a more efficient Boeing 727. The Convair was registered B-1008, and it was emaculately maintained.

H-87 was a standard UH-34 with, what appears to be, an unknown electronic sensor on the left side of the Sikorski. It also appears that the tail has been replaced at one time due to the different colors on it. The photograph was taken on December 13, 1971.

Sikorksi S-58T, XW-PHD, taxies along the ramp at Udorn AFB, Thailand, on January 22, 1972. (Ward Reimer)

This Curtis C-46D was one of the original C-46s purchased by General Chennault to start CAT. B-840 was the post-1950 Chinese registration. It was later an Air America aircraft, but it is unknown what registration or registrations were used. (Wayne Mutza)